CW00538312

Asset Transitions
Demystified

First published in Great Britain in 2018.

Copyright © Roger Wilcox 2018.

ISBN 978-1-9164288-2-9

eBook ISBN 978-1-9164288-3-6

Published by Matrixx Solutions Publishing.

www.matrixxsolutions.com

Word of Thanks

You are about to embark on an exciting journey: how to transition assets from one company to another.

I truly admire everyone I have worked with over the years who have made the Transition process a rewarding experience. Thank you!

Thank you to Peter Faulkner and Peter Miller for the opportunities you have given me. Thank you to Ivan Woodhouse, Alanna Barron, Peter Willing, Brian Miller, Mitch Flegg, John McNally and Peter Brawley for allowing me to come alongside you during your Transitions. Thank you to the many dedicated professionals who I have worked with who have made my life so easy.

By writing this book I hope to give something back:

- To demystify the Transition process.
- To help give newly appointed Transition team members a full overview of the journey they will be embarking on.
- To help standardise the way that Transitions are conducted, making it easier for lessons to be learned and shared.

After reading this book, you may wish to get further assistance with your Transition. The section titled 'Further Assistance' gives detailed information about the products and services we offer, including: Fully editable set of Transition Documentation; Provision of Training Courses; Facilitation of Transition Workshops; External input to your Transition; Personnel to support your Transition.

This can all be accessed at: www.matrixxsolutions.com

Roger Wilcox

Contents

Introduction

I've written this book to practically help anyone who will be involved in transitioning assets from one company to another to do this in an effective way. It is based on my personal experience of having successfully transitioned multi-million dollar assets in the Oil and Gas Industry to other companies and incorporates industry experience that has been gained over many years. The underlying principles and practices that are revealed in this book apply to any industry where you need to comprehensively transition assets from one company to another.

Many documents have been written about Acquisitions and Divestments, however most of the materials take you to the point where the Sale and Purchase Agreement has just been signed. Much of the information that is shared is how to secure the best price through negotiation, or how to legally and commercially structure the deal. The starting point for this book is when the Sale and Purchase Agreement is just about to be signed. It takes you through to the point when the assets are formally taken over by the Buyer.

My aim is to share how you can practically set up your Transition team and successfully transition the assets from Seller to Buyer. The importance of doing this effectively cannot be understated. A significant amount of time and effort is expended in trying to secure the best price for the assets, however, without good Transition management in place, achieving that expected value can be a significant challenge.

A Common Process for Transitions

It is a truth that no two acquisitions or divestments are the same. Each one is different, whether this be the size of the assets being sold, the experience of the Buyer to operate the assets, or the timescale for completing the Transition.

One thing is the same, though: your Transition will go through five distinct Phases and each of these will have a different characteristic:

1. Pre-announcement Preparation Phase.

2. Initiation & Ramp Up Phase.

3. Delivery Phase.

4. Drive to Completion Phase.

5. Close Out Phase.

Successfully taking the Transition through these five Phases is the domain of Programme Management.

The remainder of this book will elaborate on each of these stages.

1. Pre-announcement Preparation Phase

The Pre-announcement Preparation Phase commences at some point before the Sale and Purchase Agreement (SPA) is signed and is usually cloaked in secrecy. There may be commercial, legal and regulatory reasons (including stock market sensitivities) why such secrecy is required.

Only people who are 'in the know' that the transaction is progressing are party to it. These people will normally have signed a Confidentiality Letter, or Non-Disclosure Agreement, restricting them from disclosing information to any person or company that is not 'in the know'.

During this Phase of the Transition, the following activities are undertaken, each of which are described in more detail in the remainder of this section:

1. Establish a Steering Group for the Transition.

2. Appoint a Transition Manager.

3. Get ready to announce the sale and purchase.

4. Support the Mergers & Acquisitions Deal Team.

5. Prepare for the Initiation & Ramp Up Phase.

Establish a Steering Group for the Transition

At some point during the negotiation process, the Seller's and Buyer's Mergers & Acquisitions Deal Teams should appoint Steering Group members to form a Steering Group. These members are typically senior Executives from both the Seller and Buyer companies, who have the necessary authority to oversee the Transition and steer it towards a successful conclusion.

The role of the Steering Group is to:

- Appoint the Transition Managers and hold them accountable for delivery.
- Delegate budget and resources to the Transition Managers to enable them to deliver the Transition within agreed constraints.
- Monitor progress of the Transition and ensure that it meets Seller and Buyer corporate goals.
- Monitor the achievement of Transition strategic objectives and consider any interventions to take.
- Provide oversight of 'red' risks (those on the Transition Risk Register in the High Probability – High Impact categories) and ensure that effective plans are in place to mitigate them.
- Make decisions that enable the Transition to proceed, especially where there is an impasse between Buyer and Seller Transition teams.
- Participate in Joint Steering Group meetings and Transition Workshops.
- Approve Transition Service Agreements.
- Determine what level of independent assurance needs to be undertaken during the Transition and appoint reviewers to perform the review.
- Formally make the Go/No-Go decision: to progress with Completion on the planned date or not.

To facilitate the smooth Transition of the assets from Seller to Buyer, the Steering Group members should agree the governance structure for the Transition. This should be captured in the *How the Transition will be Governed* document, described in more detail in the Programme Management section of this book.

Appoint a Transition Manager

The next critical activity is for each company to appoint a Transition Manager and bring them 'in the know'. These individuals will manage the Transition from the point that the Sale and Purchase Agreement is signed to the Completion Date when the assets and Operatorship are formally taken over by the Buyer.

Lessons learned from previous Transitions are that Seller and Buyer should select their Transition Managers well in advance of the expected Deal Completion Date. This enables the formal Transition of the assets to commence immediately upon announcing the Sale and Purchase Agreement.

It is most common for the Transition Manager to be an employee of the respective Buyer or Seller company, although there are examples, from previous Transitions, where this hasn't been the case. The 'soft' characteristics of a good Transition Manager include the following:

- Someone who is very well respected by their organisation, who has the necessary leadership qualities to motivate Workstream Leads and keep the Transition moving forwards.
- Someone who can work closely with their Steering Group member and 'has their ear'. The strength of this relationship is very important, particularly in times when intractable issues appear, or where there are tensions between Buyer and Seller.
- Someone who can 'smell' issues and has the organisational ability to get them resolved.

The necessary 'hard' skills are that the Transition Manager has a good understanding of the overall Transition lifecycle, Programme Management practices, and lessons learned from previous Transitions. These skills can be gained by participating in other Transitions or attending an appropriate training course. The choice of your Transition Management Lead can also complement the Transition Manager, if they do not have this prior experience.

The role of the Transition Manager is to:

- Appoint Workstream Leads and the Transition Management Team and hold them accountable for delivery.
- Provide overall management of the Workstream Leads and Workstreams.
- Prepare a Transition Plan that identifies all activities and milestones that are required to be completed to successfully transition the assets from Seller to Buyer. Monitor progress and intervene when required.
- Prepare a Transition Budget that aligns with the Transition Plan and identifies all costs associated with completing the Transition. Manage delivery of costs within the agreed budget.
- Implement comprehensive Programme Management practices (including Transition Planning, Transition Budgeting, Risk Management, Progress Reporting, Document Collaboration, Communications, Programme Management Documents, and Transition Service Agreements).
- Sign-off to confirm that all Transition Deliverables have been completed.
- If requested by the Steering Group, sign-off to confirm that the assets can be safely handed over to the Buyer.

Get Ready to Announce the Sale and Purchase

A vital role that the Transition Manager can perform in the Pre-announcement Preparation Phase of the Transition is to coordinate the announcement of the sale and purchase of the assets to the incumbent workforce and external bodies.

This role could be performed by other people on the Mergers & Acquisitions Deal team, however, it is usually more efficient for the Transition Manager to do it. The Transition Manager typically has the skills necessary to develop and oversee the implementation of the Plan.

The key deliverable is a comprehensive Stakeholder Communication Plan that details, minute by minute, who is going to communicate with all the impacted internal and external parties.

It is very important that communication of the sale and purchase is conducted in a way that meets legislative requirements. The Transition Manager should work closely with the legal teams to ensure that announcements to the stock market and other legislative bodies comply with any specific requirements.

The Stakeholder Communication Plan comprises communications to External and Internal Stakeholders:

1. External Stakeholders include the following:

    o   Stock Market.
    o   Media.
    o   Relevant Industry bodies (for example, in the UK Oil and Gas Industry – the Oil & Gas Authority would be informed).
    o   Relevant Regulatory bodies (for example, in the UK – the Health & Safety Executive and the Department for Business, Energy and Industrial Strategy would be informed).
    o   Joint Venture Partners. It should be noted that, in many Joint Ventures, this notice initiates the pre-emption clause, which gives the Partners an option to buy some or all the assets in preference to the Buyer.
    o   Any major contracting companies that will be impacted by the sale and purchase. For example, in some cases the assets may be operated by a contract Operator, not by the Selling Company.

2. Internal Stakeholders include the following:

    o   Employees of the Seller and the Buyer who will be directly impacted by the sale and purchase. You should also consider how to communicate with employees who may not be in the office (due to working patterns, vacation or otherwise).

o Contract staff, including agency personnel, who are working alongside employees.

o Media teams, who will need to know how to respond to questions from external media bodies.

o Shareholder communication teams, who will need to know how to respond to questions from shareholders.

The Stakeholder Communication Plan should be written down and include the following elements:

1. A timeline from the point that the Sale and Purchase Agreement is signed until all planned communications have been completed.

2. A table listing which Stakeholder needs to be consulted, who will inform them, how they will be informed (whether verbally or by email or any other prescribed methodology), and when the communication needs to be made.

3. Pre-written statements that summarise the key aspects of the deal, that can be shared with media and external bodies. This helps to ensure that all communication is consistent and clear.

4. Pre-written guidance notes to those Managers and Team Leaders who will be informing affected employees about the sale and purchase, together with answers to expected questions.

5. A timeline for bringing additional people 'in the know' prior to the announcement. For large scale changes you may wish to make additional Managers or Team Leaders 'in the know' to help with communications to employees.

The Transition Manager should ensure that all elements of the Stakeholder Communication Plan are in place prior to announcements being made.

Once the Sale and Purchase Agreement has been signed, this triggers the commencement of Communications. The sequencing of announcements is important, and you should ensure that those that have a legislative requirement are completed first.

Every person who must make an internal or external communication should do so at the planned time. The Transition Manager will maintain an overview of how communications are progressing and ensure that all communications are completed in accordance with the Plan.

The Transition Manager also performs a coordination role: capturing feedback from completed communications and feeding this to people who still have to do their communications.

Ensure Buyer is 'present' on announcement day

Any announcement of the sale and purchase of assets will be met with shock from the incumbent workforce, particularly the people who are being 'sold'. There will be a lot of uncertainty and fear: Will they lose their jobs? What will the new company be like? What will the new company do with the asset?

One lesson learned that has helped people through this shock is for the Buyer to arrange for one of their Senior Leaders to meet with the workforce soon after the announcements. The Senior Leader should come prepared to tell a compelling story about why their company has purchased the assets, to give the workforce an idea about who their company is, and to present a personal face to the people. Key questions that they must be prepared to answer include: Why are we buying the asset? What is our vision for the future and how does the current workforce fit into that vision? What are our values?

If offshore assets are being sold, the Senior Leader should ensure that they have all the necessary Offshore Safety Certification in place, well in advance of any offshore visits.

Support the Mergers & Acquisitions Deal Team

An often-overlooked area where the Transition Manager can help the Mergers & Acquisitions Deal Team is reviewing and commenting on the Sale and Purchase Agreement, from a Transition Management perspective.

The Sale and Purchase Agreement will contain wording covering Transition topics, such as:

- The role of Workstream Leads.
- Dates when key deliverables need to be handed over from Seller to Buyer. For example: a list stating what IT applications the Seller has; or, dates when the Transition Plan and Transition Budget need to be agreed.
- Wording of Transition related concepts, such as the definition of Category A and Category B Deliverables.

The Transition Manager should be familiar with these wordings and be given an opportunity to comment on them.

Depending on the skill set and experience of the Transition Manager, they may also be able to further support the Mergers & Acquisitions Deal Team during the Pre-announcement Preparation Phase. Typical areas where they assist include: supporting the presentation of Management Presentations or helping gather or analyse data in the Data Room.

Prepare for the Initiation & Ramp Up Phase

The Transition Manager has a critical role to play in preparing for the Initiation & Ramp Up Phase of the Transition. Whilst other people are focussing on finalising the Sale and Purchase Agreement the Transition Manager can dedicate time planning what happens after it has been signed. Their role is to prepare to transfer all the Seller's people, processes, tools, systems, data and assets to the Buyer as quickly and effectively as possible.

The foundation for doing this is to:

- Establish Workstreams.
- Select Workstream Leads.
- Establish a Transition Management Team.
- Agree Transition governance and management.
- Create an initial Transition Plan.
- Focus on Critical Path activities.

Each of these will be described in more detail in the remainder of this section.

Establish Workstreams

A tried and tested way of organising the Transition is to establish Workstreams that are mirrored in both the Seller and Buyer companies. The Workstreams are accountable for identifying and transferring the processes, tools, systems and data in their area of accountability and for completing knowledge transfer. For all Transitions there are several essential workstreams:

- People.
- Safety, Health & Environment.
- IT.
- Procurement.
- Finance, Commercial and Legal.
- Document Management.

Depending on the nature of your business, there may be more. For the Oil and Gas Industry, the following Workstreams are also commonly established:

- Operational Workstreams: Operations, Maintenance, Engineering, Pipelines.
- Subsurface Workstreams: Subsurface, Drilling and Wells.
- Logistics.

The scale of your Transition will determine how many Workstreams you need to establish. However, it is not uncommon for transfers of one operating asset (onshore or offshore installation and associated support team) from one Operator to another to require around eleven Workstreams to be established. For complex asset transfers involving the transfer of multiple assets (multiple onshore or offshore installations and multiple support teams), you may require twelve to fourteen Workstreams.

Factors influencing the number of Workstreams that you require include:

- How many work areas there are within the boundaries of the Transaction that are going to be transferred.
- The expected workload in each of the work areas. As an example, if the footprint of the asset is not large and you do not have lots of storage facilities, there may only be a small work scope for the Logistics team, in which case combining this Workstream with another one, perhaps Procurement or Operations, would make sense.
- The geographical extent of your Operations. For example, if you have Operations in two completely different geographies it may be preferable to set up two Operations Workstreams, rather than trying to combine them into one.
- The organisational set up of both Buyer and Seller. For example, if both companies have combined Maintenance and Engineering teams, it would be preferable to have a single Workstream to cover these disciplines. Conversely, if both companies have separate Maintenance and Engineering teams, this may give you a strong basis for having two Workstreams.

Select Workstream Leads

Once Workstreams have been established, the Seller and Buyer need to select Workstream Leads. The fundamental role of a Workstream Lead is to transition all the defined scope within their area of responsibility from Seller to Buyer, within the specified timeline.

Their role is to:

- Prepare a Workstream Plan that identifies all activities and milestones that are required to be completed to successfully transition all the defined scope within the Workstream's area of responsibility, from Seller to Buyer. Monitor progress and intervene when required.
- Identify and secure people and resources to deliver the Workstream Plan.
- Prepare a Workstream Budget that aligns with the Plan and identifies all Workstream costs associated with completing the Transition. Manage delivery of costs within the agreed budget.
- Engage, monitor and supervise Workstream members to complete all Workstream activities in a timely manner.
- Provide support to other Workstreams to ensure delivery of cross-Workstream deliverables.
- Fulfil all Programme Management requirements (including updating plans, reports and risks registers and attending meetings and workshops).
- Sign-off to confirm that each Workstream Deliverable has been completed.

It is very important to select the right Workstream Leads. They are the individuals who will primarily be involved in the day-to-day handover of activities from Seller to Buyer and can 'make or break' the Transition.

The following factors should be considered during your selection process:

1. What level of previous Transition experience do they have? It has proven to be most effective to use people who have been involved in at least one previous Transition. Not only do they have a holistic overview of the overall Transition process, they also practically know what to do within their area of responsibility. If you do not have the luxury of using people with prior experience, then they should attend a relevant training course to boost their knowledge.

2. Can the Buyer and Seller companies release people from their own organisation to act as Workstream Leads? It is preferable to use people who are currently working for the Buyer and Seller companies. The advantage of having company employees is that they are familiar with the intricacies of how processes operate in their organisation, the applications that are in use, and the affected people that they will need to interface with during the Transition.

3. Are the Workstream Leads able to manage a team of people? Depending on the complexity of the Transition, it is likely that the Workstream Leads will need to have people working for them to complete the Deliverables. This is particularly the case for the Buyer Workstream Leads who will be involved in setting up systems, tools and processes in the new organisation.

4. Do the Workstream Leads have sufficient time available to fulfil their role? It is important not to under-resource the team. One typical mistake is to expect Workstream Leads to fulfil their role in addition to continuing with substantial 'day jobs'. This invariably leads to the quality of the Transition or the 'day job' being impacted.

To mitigate this risk, there are two commonly implemented solutions:

- o Backfill the Workstream Lead, so that they no longer need to do their 'day job' and can fully focus on the Transition.
- o Provide a 'right hand person' to the Workstream Lead who can practically fulfil a large part of the Workstream activities, with the Workstream Lead providing oversight and direction.

Prior to the announcement of the sale, the Transition Manager may not be able to speak to the potential Workstream Leads to confirm their availability, due to non-disclosure restrictions being in place. In this case, the Transition Manager may need to identify several alternative people for each role.

Workstream Leads who are 'in the ring-fence'

Once the Sale and Purchase Agreement is announced, the people who are working in the Seller's organisation that are going to be transferred to the Buyer are deemed to be 'ring-fenced'. In the UK, this means that they are subject to the Transfer of Undertakings (Protection of Employment) Regulations 2006, known colloquially as TUPE. This is an important part of UK labour law and protects employees whose business is being transferred to another company.

'Ring-fenced' employees are generally very knowledgeable about the assets that are being sold and can perform the role of Workstream Lead, providing they meet the other required qualifications. However, before appointing a 'ring-fenced' person as the Workstream Lead, you need to consider whether they will be able to continue representing the Seller company up until the point of Transition. They need to be able to make decisions that are in the best interests of the Seller company.

Practically, some Workstream Lead roles do not suit themselves to having a 'ring-fenced' employee in them, particularly those that are associated with contracts, commercial and legal agreements or company financials.

Establish a Transition Management Team

Having a high-quality Transition Management Team in place is an essential ingredient to delivering a successful Transition. Each company will typically establish a Transition Management Team that is comprised of the following roles:

- Transition Manager.
- Transition Management Lead.
- Transition Planner (this role is shared between companies).
- Communications Specialist.
- Transition Administrator.

The role of Transition Manager has previously been described, so this section will focus on the other four roles.

The Transition Management Lead is the 'right hand' to the Transition Manager and fulfils the following roles:

- Ensures that the Transition is progressing in accordance with *How the Transition will be Governed* and *How the Transition will be Managed* documents.
- Deputises for the Transition Manager when they are away.
- Enables the Transition Manager to focus on resolving higher level issues that have arisen, whilst ensuring that Workstream Leads are continually focussed on the Transition Plan, Risk Register and Action Log.
- Facilitates Transition Workshops, enabling the Transition Manager to fully participate in the events.
- Prepares progress reports.
- Resolves cross-Workstream and cross-Company issues that are affecting the Transition, as directed by the Transition Manager.

The Transition Planner is a vital member of the Transition Management Team, ensuring that an accurate Transition Plan is developed and maintained. As there is only one Transition Plan, it is customary to share one Transition Planner. The Transition Planner liaises closely with Workstream Leads on both the Buyer and Seller side and ensures that a fully integrated Plan is created. They fulfil the following roles:

- Maintain and update Workstream Plans within the selected Planning software.
- Provide ongoing coaching to Workstream Leads on all aspects of planning.
- Interrogate planning reports for signs of slippages, and to identify productivity and resource issues.
- Produce progress reports and highlight risks and opportunities to the Transition Management Team.

The role of Communications Specialist is essential in helping retain the support and enthusiasm of employees and others affected by the Transition. They fulfil the following roles:

- Develop and maintain a Communication strategy to engage the affected employee, agency and contractor workforces.
- Coordinate the development of Communication materials (newsletters, website, posters).
- Conduct surveys of the workforce, to solicit feedback from them on various aspects of the Transition that affect them, and present findings and recommendations to the Transition Managers.
- Create a 'Transition identity' to badge all Transition communications and documents. This should be sensitive to both Buyer and Seller company's visual standards.
- Ensure the accuracy of external media communications that reference the Transition.

The Transition Administrator helps ensure that the Transition progresses smoothly.

They fulfil the following roles:

- Generate and maintain Contact Lists and Holiday Trackers.
- Set up meetings.

- Set up Workshops and help ensure that all the administrative requirements (such as venue logistics) are completed.
- Perform any required administrative tasks, such as coordinating the development of the Transition Progress Report.

Depending on the size of the Transition, the roles within the Transition Management Team may be full-time or part-time.

Agree Transition Governance and Management

During the Pre-announcement Preparation Phase, the Buyer and Seller Transition Managers should agree how the Transition will be governed and managed.

Two specific deliverables should be generated:

1. *How the Transition will be Governed* document. This document is aimed at the Steering Group members and Transition Managers. It provides a framework for how they will work together and steer the Transition towards a successful conclusion.

2. *How the Transition will be Managed* document. This is a comprehensive document that describes how the Transition from Seller to Buyer will be managed. It describes the Transition Strategy, Programme Management elements and gives an overview of the Transition Workshops. It contains critical information for Workstream Leads.

Further details about each of these documents can be found in the section on Programme Management.

Create an Initial Transition Plan

At this point, the Transition Managers should generate an initial Transition Plan. You should aim to create a simple, short duration (eight week) Plan that describes the key activities that need to be completed by the Transition Teams once the Sale and Purchase Agreement has been announced.

As a guide, the Plan should include the following elements:

1. Forecast Announcement Date.

2. Early Transition Management Team activities to be completed during the Initiation & Ramp Up Phase, such as holding the Kick-Off Workshop, and Joint Transition Management Team meetings.

3. Transition Critical Path activities.

4. Any early deliverables that have been listed in the Sale and Purchase Agreement, such as the date that the Transition Plan and Transition Budget need to be issued.

Focus on Critical Path Activities

During the Pre-announcement Preparation Phase, the Transition Manager should identify what the most likely Critical Path activities of the Transition will be.

There is an opportunity to reduce the overall time taken to deliver the Transition through an early focus, from both the Seller and Buyer's Transition Teams, on progressing Critical Path activities. The Transition Manager should identify what actions can be taken prior to the Announcement of the Sale and Purchase Agreement and what actions can be taken immediately upon the Announcement being made.

Within the Oil and Gas Industry, the two most common Critical Path activities during a Transition are:

- Submission of the amended Safety Case.
- Identification and development of IT Applications and Infrastructure.

To accelerate the Safety Case submission, do the following:

- The Seller should make the existing Safety Case and all referenced documents and procedures available to the Buyer.
- The Buyer should ensure they have someone available to start writing the new company's Safety Case. The person they select should be well respected, with prior experience of successfully writing and submitting Safety Cases.

To accelerate the IT Applications and Infrastructure work, do the following:

- The Seller should prepare and provide an inventory of all IT systems (applications, software, hardware and infrastructure) that are used by the assets.
- The Buyer should populate their IT team as early as possible and start scheduling knowledge transfer sessions with the Seller's team. The purpose of these sessions is to identify the critical applications and software that will need to be purchased or replicated by Completion Date.

A further early activity that should be completed is to establish Transition Cost Codes. This will enable the Workstream Leads to set up contracts and start progressing Critical Path activities.

Depending on who is 'in the know', it may be possible to undertake these activities prior to Announcement day. If this is not possible, then it should be an early focus of the Initiation & Ramp Up Phase.

2. Initiation & Ramp Up Phase

The Initiation & Ramp Up Phase commences as soon as the Sale and Purchase Agreement has been signed. This Phase is characterised by:

1. Dealing with a Shocked Organisation.

2. Populating and Onboarding the Transition teams.

3. Finalising Terms of Reference Documents and Building the Transition Plan.

4. Onboarding people who join the Transition teams late.

This section of the book will give you a more detailed understanding of each of these elements.

Dealing with a Shocked Organisation

The first activity that takes place in the Initiation & Ramp Up Phase is the announcement of the deal. Announcements often commence before 8 am, to ensure that the Buyer and Seller comply with stringent stock exchange rules and regulations.

With modern media practices, it is highly likely that Twitter, social media and news services will be buzzing with the contents of the press release soon after news of a major acquisition or divestment is released. So, expect and plan on your employees being aware of the transaction even before they arrive into work in the morning.

As part of your Stakeholder Communication Plan, your leadership team should be primed to hold meetings with employees and key affected people as soon as practically possible. At this stage, there will often be a sense of shock and disbelief, and sensitivity is required when dealing with people. Key questions that you must be prepared to answer include: Why are we selling the asset? What does it mean to me – am I being sold with the asset too? Who is the buying company? What's the timescale for transitioning over? What are the next steps?

It's advisable to have the Buyer meet your employees and key affected people soon after the Announcement. The Buyer should come armed with a compelling story to tell the workforce. Primary topics to cover include: Why are we buying the asset? What is our vision for the future and how does the current workforce fit into that vision? What are our values? Above all, these interactions are meant to reassure the unsettled workforce, so they need to be led by your most senior leaders; this is not a task to be delegated.

People each react differently to the announcement of the asset that they're working on being sold. Some people become despondent and more introverted than usual and need time to process the news, while some people can quickly 'get their head around' the change and get back to their day job. However people react, you need to be prepared for this.

Key questions you need to answer are:

- Do you need to make independent help available to people who need assistance processing the change?
- Do you need to change working patterns (stop or reduce work or higher risk activities) on the day of the announcement, as people may be distracted more than usual?

It is advisable to have high leadership presence around the workforce during the first couple of weeks post-Announcement. Their role is to answer questions, to pay attention to their teams and see how they are coping with the news, and to bring comfort and hope to them.

Remember that it is not only employees that are affected, but also agency personnel and contractors who work for the affected assets. This community will have different questions, including: Will my contract continue when the assets change hands? Will my terms and conditions change? What are the next steps?

Failing to communicate well with this community has the potential to adversely affect an individual's performance (due to being distracted by the uncertainty). For agency personnel, who do not have the certainty of continued employment that contractors working for a service provider have, there is an increased risk of resignations, potentially leading to gaps within the organisation.

At this stage of the Transition, many of the contractual-type questions that people have are likely to be unanswerable. To help alleviate concerns, you should be prepared to inform people of the forward timeline for the Transition and reassure them that one of the Workstreams (probably Procurement Workstream) will be focussed on this area.

Populating and Onboarding the Transition Teams

Once the Sale and Purchase has been announced, the Transition properly commences. The priority task is to fill all the vacant Workstream Lead roles.

As stated earlier, the selection of these individuals can 'make or break' the Transition. You should ensure that the Workstream Leads you select have time to perform the role, have previous experience of Transitions, and are able to manage a team of individuals.

Kick-Off Workshop

As soon as practical after the announcement of the Sale and Purchase, and once most of the Seller and Buyer Workstream Leads are available, you should aim to get the combined Transition teams together and do the following:

1. Start building collaborative relationships between the Seller and Buyer teams.

2. Present an overview of the assets being sold and any commercial aspects that Workstream Leads need to be aware of.

3. Ensure that everyone understands their role and the Programme Management practices that will be used throughout the Transition.

4. Develop Terms of Reference for each Workstream.

The best way of achieving this is to hold a Kick-Off Workshop.

The following section of the book will give a detailed breakdown of what you should include within this Workshop, particularly the following:

1. Background on the Commercial Deal.

2. Objectives and Principles of Transition.

3. Role of the Workstream Lead.

4. Programme Management Practices.

5. Workstream Terms of Reference documents.

Background on the Commercial Deal

Before getting into the mechanics of how the Transition will take place, it is helpful for Workstream Leads to be given additional background to the assets being sold and to some of the commercial aspects contained within the Sale and Purchase Agreement and Transfer of Operatorship Agreements. Remember that the Workstream Leads may not be familiar with the assets or commercial aspects of the Transition.

Specific topics to address should include:

- What is the full listing of assets being sold (the scope of the deal)? Ensure that you not only include the obvious assets, such as platforms, pipelines and terminals, but also less obvious ones, such as offices, warehouses, inventory.
- What are the boundaries? You need to clearly identify the extent of licence areas for the subsurface team and the extent of pipelines for the engineering and operations teams.
- What are the Conditions Precedent of the deal? Workstream Leads need to be aware of all the conditions that must take place before Completion Date. In the UK Oil and Gas industry, typical Conditions Precedent include:

    - Receipt of all relevant consents and approvals from the UK Oil and Gas Authority for the Seller to stop being the Operator and the Buyer to become Operator.
    - Written confirmation from Partners that they have waived their pre-emption rights, or alternatively that the window for Partners to exercise their pre-emption rights has passed.
    - Confirmation from both Transition Managers that Operatorship can transfer safely from Seller to Buyer.

- What are the key obligations contained within the commercial agreements that the Transition team need to be aware of? For example, here are a list of some of the common obligations that may have been incorporated into the Sale and Purchase Agreement:

    - Issue a Transition Plan and associated Transition Budget, identifying the key milestones and activities necessary to complete the Transition.
    - Provide a full listing of all IT applications and infrastructure that the Seller has.
    - Provide a full listing of all seismic contracts that the Seller owns.

- o Consult with the Buyer in relation to any material decision affecting the Assets.

- Does the Buyer have any specific biases that Workstream Leads need to be aware of? For example, have they stated a desire to use 'off the shelf' IT applications or 'in-house' equivalents? Do they intend to retain existing contracts or migrate to their own suppliers?

Objectives and Principles of Transition

It is helpful to clearly communicate what some of the overarching objectives are for the Transition period.

The following ones are applicable within the Oil and Gas Industry:

- Maintain safe and effective operations.
- Ensure that the Transition does not have a detrimental impact on business performance: safety, integrity or financials.
- Transfer Seller personnel to Buyer as smoothly as possible, in accordance with legislative requirements.
- Complete the Transition on time and within budget.
- Communicate well with everyone affected by the Sale and Purchase.

I have also found it beneficial to establish clear principles that set forth how the Transition teams will behave, and communicate these at the Kick-Off Workshop. These principles provide a foundation for Workstream Lead behaviours:

- **Safety First**: safety, health and environmental performance of the asset should always be prioritised over Transition activity.
- **Keep people informed**: work hard to communicate with everyone who is affected by the Transition. It's equally as important to transition people's 'hearts and minds' as it is to transition over the assets.

- **Maintain security of personal information**: such information is subject to strict legal guidelines and will only be shared in accordance with statutory obligations.
- **Minimise change**: focus on transitioning the asset from Seller to Buyer 'as is'. Avoid the temptation for Workstream Leads to try to fix all of the Seller's systems and processes that are perceived to be 'wrong' during the Transition.
- **Seek help early and escalate issues**: Don't waste time trying to resolve issues yourselves: escalate to the Transition Managers. They can escalate issues to the Steering Group, if required.
- **Do the right work at the right time**: Plan your activities and then 'work your plan', doing activities when they need to be done rather than rushing to do everything at once.

Role of the Workstream Lead

The Kick-Off Workshop is the perfect time for the Transition Managers to reiterate what the role of the Workstream Lead is. This may be the first Transition for some of your Workstream Leads and this information will help build their understanding of the role and accelerate them up the learning curve.

The fundamental role of a Workstream Lead is to transition all the defined scope within their area of responsibility, from Seller to Buyer, within the specified timeline. You can use the following role statements:

- Prepare a Workstream Plan that identifies all activities and milestones that are required to be completed to successfully transition all the defined scope within the Workstream's area of responsibility from Seller to Buyer. Monitor progress and intervene when required.
- Identify and secure people and resources to deliver the Workstream Plan.
- Prepare a Workstream Budget that aligns with the Plan and identifies all Workstream costs associated with completing

the Transition. Manage delivery of costs within the agreed budget.

- Engage, monitor and supervise Workstream members to complete all Workstream activities in a timely manner.
- Provide support to other Workstreams to ensure delivery of cross-Workstream deliverables.
- Fulfil all Programme Management requirements (including updating plans, reports and risks registers and attending meetings and workshops).
- Sign-off to confirm that each Workstream Deliverable has been completed.

Programme Management Practices

One of the primary objectives of the Kick-Off Workshop is to ensure that everyone understands the programme management practices that will be used throughout the Transition. I recommend spending quality time during the Kick-Off Workshop talking through the practices that will be used and answering questions about them. You can issue copies of the *How the Transition will be Managed* document to all your Workstream Leads as an aide memoire.

The section on Programme Management will give you a detailed understanding of practices that are commonly applied to managing Transitions in the Oil and Gas Industry. During the Kick-Off Workshop, cover each of the elements in sufficient detail that your Workstream Leads know what they need to do.

The following checklist can be used to ensure that you have all the necessary presentation materials available:

- ☐ Transition Governance.
- ☐ Transition Planning.
- ☐ Transition Budgeting.
- ☐ Risk Management.
- ☐ Progress Reporting.
- ☐ Document Collaboration.
- ☐ Communications.
- ☐ Programme Management Documents.
- ☐ Transition Service Agreements.

Workstream Terms of Reference Documents

I like to think that the foundations for a successful Transition have been laid once the Workstream Leads have been given an overview of the assets being sold, any commercial aspects that they need to be aware of, their role in the Transition and the programme management practices that are going to be used.

Now it is time to get down to work and start developing Workstream Terms of Reference documents. These documents are the fundamental building block to developing a robust Transition Plan and Budget. They typically contain the following sections:

1. Contact Information for Workstream Leads and Workstream team members.

2. Scopes of Work for the Workstream.

3. Deliverables and Key Interdependencies with other Workstreams.

4. What work is considered 'out of scope' for the Workstream.

5. Workstream Resource and Budget Estimates for Buyer and Seller.

6. How the Workstream team will work together.

7. Any other points for consideration.

From a facilitation perspective, I always want to ensure that there is sufficient time built into the Kick-Off Workshop to enable Workstream Leads to have deep discussions during the development of the Terms of Reference documents. I request Workstream Leads to come to the Kick-Off Workshop armed with their laptop, so that they can make live updates to their document.

One of the potential 'bear traps' that people fall into is focussing on activities that need to be done, rather than identifying Deliverables that need to be completed. If people fall into this trap, they leave the Workshop with long lists of things to do. They also run the risk of missing out on key Scopes of Work that need to be transferred from Seller to Buyer. To avoid this trap, you should reiterate what the differences between Scopes of Work, Deliverables and Activities are, preferably with examples from your own experience. It is very helpful to make this as visual as possible to the Workstream Leads.

I recommend giving your Workstream Leads pre-populated Terms of Reference templates, or copies from previous Transitions, as this will provide a spring board from which to start the discussions. The downside of doing this is that some people switch off and don't spend sufficient time thinking through the specific details of the Transition. To avoid this trap, you may find it beneficial to give the Workstream Leads some time to talk about the Scopes of Work before handing out the pre-populated templates. This approach enables them to use their imagination and creativity and then build on this once the templates are handed out.

Before closing the workshop, do set a date when you expect to receive completed Terms of Reference documents back from Workstream Leads.

By the end of the Workshop, people are typically quite tired, having expended a lot of energy. You will know if you have achieved your goal of starting to build collaborative relationships if people continue talking to one another after you have formally closed the Workshop.

Top tips for your Facilitator during the Kick-Off Workshop include:

- Ensure that you go around the room and let everyone introduce themselves. There are numerous techniques for doing this, but as a minimum, make sure that everyone lets the others in the room know their name and what their role is in the Transition.
- Don't skimp on breaks. Avoid the temptation to reduce the duration of comfort and lunch breaks. These are times when you want people talking to each other and building relationships.
- Have name badges printed out that people wear throughout the day. The feedback that I've received is that this helps people memorise the names of the people they're working with. Always have a sheet of sticky label paper and a felt tip pen available to enable you to write up an impromptu name badge if an unexpected person joins the meeting.

Finalise Documents and Build the Transition Plan

Soon after completing the Kick-Off Workshop, the Transition Management Team need to focus on finalising Terms of Reference documents and building the Transition Plan, in conjunction with Workstream Leads.

Finalise Terms of Reference Documents

Once the completed Terms of Reference documents have been received from the Workstream Leads, the Transition Management Team should cross-check them. The reasons for doing this cross-check are:

- To identify missing Scopes of Work.
- To highlight duplicated Scopes of Work and to identify cross-Workstream themes that may require more focussed conversations to clarify accountabilities.
- To ensure that Scopes of Work that Workstreams have identified as being outside their remit are located on another Workstream's Terms of Reference document.

Some practical steps for conducting this cross-check are:

1. Create a 'cross-check matrix' by writing down each of the Workstream's Scopes of Works side by side on a single sheet of paper. I create an Excel spreadsheet to do this.

2. Go through the matrix and highlight in colour where the Scopes of Work are duplicated. Highlight the duplications and agree which Workstream is going to take the lead.

3. Highlight anything missing, from your experience or following a review of matrices used on previous Transitions.

4. Review what each Workstream has identified as being 'out of scope' for them to deliver. I then recommend that you sit down individually with each of your Workstream Leads and find a home for all the 'out of scope' topics.

Once you have completed this review, the Terms of Reference documents should be updated to reflect any changes to accountability for delivering Scopes of Work. These updated documents now become the building block for finalising Deliverables and for creating Workstream Plans.

Build the Transition Plan

Once the Scopes of Work have been finalised, the next step can be taken: build the Transition Plan.

The Transition Plan integrates all the individual Workstream level activities into one overall Plan. Generating a high-quality, fully-integrated Transition Plan is an essential element of any Transition, for the following reasons:

- It provides your Workstream Leads with a structured plan to follow. This helps them to focus on delivering all their activities by the Completion Date. It also helps them to complete activities at the right time and in the right order.
- It enables you to generate a High Level Strategic Plan for the Transition. This document can be used to communicate

progress of the Transition to the Workforce, Workstream Leads and the Steering Group.

- It helps ensure that cross-Workstream activities are identified and appropriately resourced.
- It provides a tangible basis for assessing how the Transition is progressing.

To create a fully integrated Transition Plan, complete the following seven steps:

- Step 1. Identify Scopes of Work for each Workstream.
- Step 2. Identify Deliverables for each Scope of Work.
- Step 3. Categorise Deliverables as Category A or B.
- Step 4. Identify Activities that need to be completed.
- Step 5. Create the Transition Plan.
- Step 6. Identify Interdependencies.
- Step 7. Use the Plan to manage Transition delivery.

These steps are broken down into more detail in the Programme Management section of the book.

Workstream Leads will generate their Workstream Plans, in conjunction with the Transition Planner. The Transition Planner will incorporate all the Workstream activities into the Planning tool and will generate a series of reports (described in more detail in the Programme Management section of the book):

1. High Level Strategic Plan.

2. Deliverable Run-Down Curve.

3. Transition Plan.

4. Workstream Plans.

5. Transition S-Curve.

Onboarding People who Join the Transition Late

It is inevitable that people will join the Transition team after the Kick-Off Workshop has been held. There is a real risk that these people waste valuable time trying to find out how the Transition works.

A best practice is to have a simple induction process in place for newcomers to the Transition, which includes the following:

1. Sit down with them and review the materials that were used in the Kick-Off Workshop, particularly those focussing on the Transition principles and programme management practices.

2. Issue them with a copy of the document *How the Transition will be Managed*.

3. Hold a one-to-one session with them to discuss and agree specific Roles and Responsibilities.

4. Issue them with a copy of the latest Terms of Reference, Transition Plan, Risk Register and Transition Progress Report that is relevant to their role, for their information.

3. Delivery Phase

The Delivery Phase of the Transition commences once the Workstream Leads have had time to sufficiently develop their Workstream Plans. It starts with a Plan Review Workshop, where the Workstream Leads collectively review and challenge all Workstream Plans. It concludes after the Mid-Transition Review Workshop has been held. This Phase of the Transition is where the bulk of the Transition work will be completed by the Workstream Leads.

During the Delivery Phase, the Transition Management Team focuses on the following:

1.   Testing the Transition Plan.

2.   Freezing the Transition Plan and Transition Budget.

3.   Enabling Workstream Leads to get work done.

4.   Holding the Mid-Transition Review Workshop.

Each of these are broken down into more detail in this section of the book.

Testing the Transition Plan

The goal of the Plan Review Workshop is to collaboratively review and challenge all Workstream Plans. From a behavioural perspective, this is a critical event, where the intent is to change mindsets of Workstream Leads from 'Planning with a bit of Execution' to 'Focussed delivery of the Plan'. When Workstream Leads leave this Workshop, they should be firmly focussed on Delivery: delivering all activities on their Plan within the required timeframe.

There are seven primary objectives of this Workshop:

1. Conduct a thorough review of all Workstream Plans.

2. Ensure that each Workstream has clarity on the planned activities they need to complete to achieve the agreed Deliverables.

3. Ensure that interdependencies between Workstreams are identified and incorporated into the Plan.

4. Develop Risk Registers for each Workstream.

5. Ensure that Workstream Leads understand the requirements for regular Transition reporting.

6. Share cross-Workstream information with attendees.

7. Continue building collaborative relationships between teams.

Top tips for your Facilitator include:

- Before the Workshop, identify Workstream's that have critical information that needs to be shared across all Workstreams and ask them to present this. For typical Transitions within the Oil and Gas Industry, this will involve presentations from the following Workstreams: IT, Document Management, and People.
- Before the Workshop, ensure that the location you choose to hold the Workshop has sufficient wall space for you to put up Workstream Plans. You will also want to ensure that the selected establishment is happy for you to use Blu Tack, or equivalent.
- Do print out copies of each Workstream's Plans, preferably in A1 format.
- On the day, do get the Buyer or Seller's most senior person to bring a sense of urgency to the meeting. You can successfully do this by getting them to speak early during the Workshop and highlight what percentage through the Transition you currently are. Ask them to reiterate the

importance of transitioning from Planning into Delivering the Plan.

By the time of the Plan Review Workshop, your Workstream Leads should be very familiar with the Plan and the regular Plan update process. However, this is an opportune time for the Transition Planner to feedback any learnings or improvements that need to be made by the Workstream Leads.

The bulk of the Workshop should focus on reviewing Workstream Plans. A very successful process to employ is:

1. Post Workstream Plans around the room, in five or six 'stations'.

2. Ask Workstream Leads to appoint someone to remain at their 'station' to feedback to the other Workstream Leads.

3. The remaining people divide into equal-sized groups and position themselves at one of the 'stations'.

4. At each 'station', the Workstream Lead gives the assembled group around them an overview of their Plan, highlighting such things as the key scopes of work they will deliver and interdependencies with other Workstreams. The assembled group should be encouraged to identify any issues that they can see with the Plan.

5. After approximately 10-15 minutes at one station, the assembled groups should rotate around to the next 'station' and repeat the process.

This process is very interactive and enables Workstream Plans to be closely scrutinised. My preference is for the assembled groups to write down any issues or improvements that they see on post-it notes and hand these to the Workstream Lead who is manning the 'station'. This enables all the feedback to be collated and later incorporated into the Workstream Plans.

For Transitions where there are ten or more workstreams, it works well to split these up into two sessions with a break in the middle.

During the break, the facilitation team should take down the first set of Plans and put up the second set. Having a break at this point maintains the energy in the room.

There is one exception to the above practice. For those Workstreams that significantly impact all Workstreams, I like them to present their Plans in a plenary session, rather than having them as a 'station'. This gives the opportunity for questions that impact multiple Workstreams to be asked and addressed. The two Workstreams that often fall into this category are the IT Workstream and the Document Management Workstream.

Another primary objective of the Plan Review Workshop is to develop Risk Registers for each Workstream. I like to do this in the Workshop as it enables the Workstream Leads to develop a shared understanding of the definitions of risk, impact and probability that they will be using.

The session on risks is most effective when you do the following:

1. Describe why risk management is important to the Transition and how risks will be managed through the Transition.

2. Review the Risk Registers that you will be using and ensure that all Workstream Leads understand the definitions that are used and any required fields that need to be completed.

3. Present 'good' and 'bad' risk descriptors and consequences.

4. Break the attendees into Workstreams and ask them to conduct a risk assessment for their Workstream. The Transition Management Team should be present during this time to answer questions and to help ensure that Workstream Leads fully complete the required fields on the Risk Register.

5. Once each Workstream has completed their Risk Register, solicit feedback to determine whether any risks require significant input from other Workstreams to mitigate them.

6. Describe the next steps that Workstream Leads need to take. This usually consists of: getting the Workstream Leads to finalise any outstanding issues and, submitting their Risk Register for inclusion in the overall Transition Risk Register.

Now that the Workstream Leads have populated their Risk Registers, it is an opportune time to reiterate the importance of regular Progress reporting and to define the expectation of Workstream Leads to:

- Update Workstream Plans.
- Update Progress Reports.
- Update Risk Registers.

By the time of the Plan Review Workshop, most Workstream Leads will be familiar with working with one another. However, it is still important to continue building collaborative relationships. Throughout the Workshop, you should ensure that you don't reduce the time allocated to breaks and lunches. It is often a good point in the Transition to bring the teams together for a meal in the evening. If you decide to do this, then I would recommend arranging something buffet-style, where people can roam around and easily speak to others, rather than being locked into a seat, only speaking to a few people around them.

Freezing the Transition Plan and Transition Budget

Immediately following the Plan Review Workshop, the Transition Planner should work with each of the Workstream Leads to incorporate any feedback that they received into the Plan. Once this exercise has been completed, the Transition Planner can finalise and publish the Transition Plan.

This Plan is sometimes referred to as 'the Initial Baseline Transition Plan': it provides a starting point from which Plan progress can be measured. It forms one of the two lines on the Transition S-Curve and helps give a visual indication of whether the Transition is on track to complete by the targeted Completion date, or not.

Given the nature of Transitions, the plan evolves, depending on what discoveries are made by Workstream Leads, or what unexpected issues are encountered. It is not helpful to apply rigid project management planning practices to the Transition. Therefore, your Transition Planner needs to determine the optimal time to re-baseline the Plan. The priority is to enable Workstream Leads to identify when they are behind schedule on completing their planned activities.

The Transition Budget should be finalised at the same time the Transition Plan is finalised. The Workstream Leads should ensure that all the costs in the Budget correspond with the planned activities they will undertake and the planned resources they will have.

It is customary for the first Steering Group meeting following the Plan Review Workshop to review and approve the Transition Plan and Budget.

Enabling Workstream Leads to get Work Done

The Delivery Phase of the Transition is where the bulk of the Transition work will be completed by the Workstream Leads. It is imperative that, during this Phase, the Transition Management Team focuses on enabling them to get work done as efficiently as possible.

From a Transition Management Team perspective, you should focus on the following:

- Ramping up delivery of the Workstream Leads.
- Performance Managing Critical Path activities.
- Surfacing and resolving issues.
- Getting work done at site.
- Preparing for Workforce Training and Familiarisation.
- Managing involvement of people in the 'ring-fence'.
- Recruiting people for the Buyer's Day 1 organisation.

The following section of the book will elaborate on each of these in more detail.

Ramping up Delivery of the Workstream Leads

The Transition Management Team need to ensure that Workstream Leads can ramp up delivery of their activities. It is essential to confirm with each Workstream Lead that they have the following:

- Line of sight to bringing on board sufficient people to complete the required Workstream activities. Failure to get people on board at the required time has a knock-on impact to the Workstream: the work starts accumulating and it gets increasingly difficult to get on top of it.
- Sufficient budget to enable the Workstream Lead to complete all their Workstream activities. If there is a 'bust' at this stage of the Transition that cannot be resolved by the Transition Managers, it will need to be highlighted to the Steering Group. They will decide whether to increase the budget to enable the work to be completed, or alternatively, agree what scope of work will not be completed and accept any associated risks to the Transition due to making this decision.

The Transition Management Team should also review and challenge what assumptions Workstream Leads have made about the profile of resourcing their teams. Workstream Leads may need to employ additional people for short periods of time, to deal with peaks of activity.

The Transition Management Team should keep Workstream Leads focused on progressing planned activities, rather than spending time trying to get the plan right.

Performance Managing Critical Path Activities

By the time that the Delivery Phase commences, there should be clarity on what the Critical Path activities of the Transition are.

A vital role of the Transition Manager is to ensure that the relevant Workstream Leads are performance managing delivery of these activities. This is typically undertaken by having frequent check-ins on progress of the Critical Path activities. Early identification of issues enables actions to be taken to resolve them.

Surfacing and Resolving Issues

During the early part of the Delivery Phase, it is crucial to start getting into a regular rhythm of Programme Management, if you haven't done so already. This gives Workstream Leads a formal opportunity to surface issues for resolution, in meetings and reports. Further details of each of these are contained within the Programme Management section of this book.

1. Hold Company-Specific Workstream Lead Progress Review meetings.

    My bias is to have one-to-one check-ins with critical Workstream Leads (those that have lots of activities, or where their activities are on the Critical Path – such as IT Workstream and Safety, Health and Environment Workstream) and then divide the remaining Workstream Leads into groups of similar Workstreams (such as Operations, Engineering and Maintenance).

    During the Delivery Phase, it is highly likely that issues will emerge during these meetings. Some of these will get resolved by the Workstream Leads, however there will be some that need help from the Transition Management Team to resolve. During these meetings, you should listen out for common concerns that are raised by different Workstreams: these may point to an overarching issue that needs to be discussed and resolved.

2. Hold Joint Transition Team Meetings.

    These meetings are attended by all members of the Buyer's and Seller's Transition Management Teams and all Workstream Leads. The meeting provides an opportunity for Workstream Leads to raise issues that need to be resolved, particularly cross-Workstream issues. The meetings work best when they are limited to about one-hour durations, therefore the focus is not on resolving issues that are raised, but agreeing Specific, Measurable and Time-bound actions to resolve them after the meeting.

3. Complete the Transition Progress Report.

    Workstream Leads should take the opportunity to highlight any issues that they need help resolving in the Transition Progress Report. This document is a formal written report of progress that is updated on a regular basis.

Escalation Process for Resolving issues

The escalation process for resolving issues that are raised should be:

1. Workstream Leads. In the first instance, they should work together to resolve issues. It is sometimes tempting for the Transition Management Team to step in and try and resolve issues at this level, however, you should avoid that temptation. Instead, devolve accountability for decision making down to the Workstream Leads. This will make the whole Transition smoother and will prevent the Transition Management Team becoming a bottle-neck for decisions being made.

2. Transition Managers. Where Workstream Leads cannot resolve issues among themselves, or where there are issues that cross multiple Workstreams, the Transition Managers should work to resolve them.

3. Steering Group. In some instances, there are issues that the Transition Managers cannot resolve, particularly where resolution of the issue may require support or resources from within the Buyer and Seller's companies. These issues need to be escalated to the Steering Group for resolution.

Getting Work Done at Site

At some stage during the Transition, there will be a requirement to perform physical work at site: whether onshore or offshore. Examples could include: installing firewalls, new cabling, servers, power and local area networks.

During the Delivery Phase of the Transition, the Transition Management Team should ensure that all Workstream Leads have a good understanding of how to get work done at site.

This may include such things as:

- Working with the Site Planning team to get the activities added to the Site Plan.
- Preparing Workpacks.
- Participating in Management of Change reviews.
- Participating in Control of Work reviews with the site.
- Ensuring that everyone who will be working on site have the required certification and safety training.

It is helpful to publish these requirements and identify any specific deadlines that must be met and, any site contacts that Workstream Leads need to liaise with.

Preparing for Workforce Training and Familiarisation

During the Delivery Phase of the Transition, there is a requirement for the Buyer to identify what level of training and familiarisation will need to be given to people to enable them to perform effectively on Day 1: the day after Completion Date.

Training is defined as teaching someone a skill: for example, how to use a specific business application. Training can be done in classrooms; virtually, using online facilities or having 'floor-walkers' (experts on hand to provide on-the-job training).

Familiarisation is defined as giving someone knowledge or understanding about something. For example, giving people who are transferring from the Seller to the Buyer an overview of the Buyer's

Safety, Health and Environmental expectations or Personnel policies and practices.

The level of training and familiarisation that is given will depend on the following factors:

1. The level of change to tools (business applications that are used), business processes and procedures. In most Transitions, the bias is to minimise change.

2. The number of new people that are expected to be recruited to start working with the Buyer company on Day 1.

3. How much time the Buyer and Seller dedicates for training and familiarisation. There is often a tension between the Buyer and Seller: the Seller is still operating the site and wants to minimise the impact of change on their people, whilst the Buyer wants to ensure that everyone will be able to perform their role on Day 1.

Given that Training and Familiarisation impacts all Workstreams, a best practice to coordinate this is to do the following:

1. Appoint one of the Buyer's Workstream Leads to act as Training and Familiarisation Coordinator. This individual will have the role of coordinating the overall development of the Training and Familiarisation Plan.

2. Give all Workstream Leads the responsibility of identifying what tools, processes and procedures have changed, within their area of accountability, and identifying whether training or familiarisation is required. This should be fed into the Training and Familiarisation Coordinator.

3. Workstream Leads will coordinate the development of any required training materials in their area of responsibility.

A successful outcome is one in which people can perform the key elements of their role on Day 1.

Managing Involvement of People in the 'ring-fence'

Once the Sale and Purchase Agreement is announced, the people who are working in the Seller's organisation that are going to be transferred to the Buyer are deemed to be 'ring-fenced'. In the UK, this means that they are subject to the Transfer of Undertakings (Protection of Employment) Regulations 2006, known colloquially as TUPE. This is an important part of UK labour law and protects employees whose business is being transferred to another company.

During the Delivery Phase of the Transition, there is likely to be an increasing number of 'ring-fenced' people that get involved with the Transition. It is worth ensuring that these people understand their obligations to the Seller and do not stray into making decisions or doing things which are the Buyer's accountability. This can be done by writing a *Rules of Engagement* document.

This will define such things as:

1. The Seller's role in the Transition: to collate, prepare and handover data, documents, processes, procedures and business systems. To complete 'knowledge transfer', providing clarification to the Buyer on all the above.

2. The Buyer's role in the Transition: to receive what is handed over and incorporate it into their processes and business systems. They need to make decisions that are consistent with how they will operate the asset in the future.

3. What Seller's personnel can and cannot do and say. For example, they should not make any decisions on behalf of the Buyer, even if they are going to be in a decision-making capacity in the future, once they become employees of the Buyer. The Buyer needs to understand the obligations and responsibilities it will take on as Owner and Operator of the asset.

Recruiting People for Buyer's Day 1 Organisation

One of the roles that falls into the People Workstream is to coordinate the development of an organisation within the Buyer's company to host the acquired assets. This organisation needs to be robust to fully operate the acquired assets on Day 1 of the new organisation: immediately upon Completion of the Transition.

Once the organisational design has been completed, there will be a requirement to recruit people to fill vacancies.

Although it is tempting to leave the recruitment of people until later in the Transition, to minimise costs, this is a false economy. In the UK it is commonplace for company employees to have a notice period of up to three months, and agency personnel may have notice periods of 2–4 weeks. Therefore, starting the recruitment phase early ensures that you can complete interviews, make an offer and complete the recruitment process prior to Completion Date.

Having people in the Buyer's organisation in place early also helps with completing Knowledge Transfer from the Seller's organisation.

Holding the Mid-Transition Review Workshop

An important event to hold during the Delivery Phase is the Mid-Transition Review Workshop. The Workshop is timed to occur at approximately the midpoint of the Transition. It has the following objectives:

1. Focus teams on the end-point: Completion Date.

2. Ensure that everyone is clear on the formal process for signing off Workstream Deliverables.

3. Review all outstanding risks on the Risk Register and ensure that mitigating activities are being progressed.

4. Conduct a thorough review of all Workstream Plans. Ensure that each Workstream has clarity on the planned activities they need to complete to achieve the agreed Deliverables.

5. Review and confirm Training and Familiarisation Plan.

6. Discuss topics that impact multiple Workstreams.

Further details on each of these topics is given in the remainder of this section of the book.

Focus Teams on the end-point: Completion Date

Since the Plan Review Workshop, the Workstream Leads have been focussed on completing the myriad of planned activities on their Workstream Plans. However, it is usual for the Plan that was presented at the Plan Review Workshop to have grown, as Workstream Leads identify new activities that need to be done during discovery sessions between Seller and Buyer. The Mid-Transition Review Workshop is specifically intended to change the mindsets of the Workstream Leads, to get them to focus on the end of the Transition. This shift is important as, once this mindset is locked in, Workstream Leads become more energised to close out activities and not add new activities. All of this helps drive towards a successful completion of the Transition.

Like the Plan Review Workshop, it is helpful for the Buyer or Seller's most senior person to bring a sense of urgency to the meeting. It is also an appropriate time to share your High Level Strategic Plan and show which activities have been completed so far.

Process for signing off Workstream Deliverables

One of the ways of getting people to focus on the end-point of the Transition is to start talking about Completion Date during the early part of the Workshop.

This can be achieved by giving Workstream Leads a good understanding of the sign-off process: when they will need to start signing off their Deliverables, and what they will need to sign.

This is an appropriate time to bring out examples of the actual forms that will be used at sign-off and ask the Workstream Leads to review and amend any of their Deliverables.

Outstanding Risks on the Risk Register

An essential element of the Mid-Transition Review Workshop is to review the remaining 'red' risks (those that are high impact and high probability of occurrence) on Workstream Risk Registers.

A straightforward way of reviewing these risks is to ask each Workstream Lead to share what 'red' risks there are on their Risk Register and the status of mitigating them. Workstream Leads should be encouraged to be transparent and give as realistic a picture of the remaining risk as possible.

During their presentation, Workstream Leads should particularly highlight where they require support from other Workstreams to complete mitigating actions. In those instances, where other Workstreams are required to support completion of actions, the Transition Management Team should ensure that the required mitigating actions are Specific, Measurable and that the supporting Workstream Lead takes ownership of the action.

Conduct a Thorough Review of Workstream Plans

The bulk of the Mid-Transition Review Workshop should focus on reviewing Workstream Plans. The practice that was employed during the Plan Review meeting can be successfully employed again:

1. Post Workstream Plans around the room, in five or six 'stations'.

2. Ask Workstream Leads to appoint someone to remain at their 'station' to feedback to the other Workstream Leads.

3. The remaining people divide into equal-sized groups and position themselves at one of the 'stations'.

4. At each 'station', the Workstream Lead gives the assembled group around them an overview of their Plan, highlighting such things as the key scopes of work they will deliver and interdependencies with other Workstreams. The assembled group should be encouraged to identify any issues that they can see with the Plan. This is normally a very interactive session.

5. After approximately 10-15 minutes at one 'station' the assembled groups should rotate around to the next 'station' and repeat the process.

It is very helpful if the assembled groups write down any issues or improvements that they see on post-it notes and hand these to the Workstream Lead who is manning the 'station'. This enables all the feedback to be collated and later incorporated into the Workstream Plans.

The Workstream Leads should focus on three aspects of the Plan:

1. Has the Plan fully identified all the demand for asset personnel to support the Transition? This often shows up on Plans in the form of 'Training' requirements, 'User Acceptance Testing' of software or 'Company Inductions' or similar.

2. Are there any activities in the final month of the Transition that can be accelerated? It is much better to complete tasks early and cruise to a smooth transition on Completion Day rather than frantically rushing around trying to get everything finished in the final days or weeks.

3. Are there any activities that are at risk of not being completed by Completion Date? If so, this is the time to identify them and start developing contingency plans.

The methodology identified above works very well for the majority of Workstreams, however, you may find it more efficient for the IT Workstream to present their Plan to all the Workstream Leads at the same time. This gives the IT Workstream Leads the opportunity to present their Plan, but also to talk more specifically about the Freeze

Calendar and Cutover Plan and any support that they will need from the other Workstreams to conduct User Acceptance Testing.

Training and Familiarisation Plan

During the Delivery Phase of the Transition, there is a requirement for the Buyer to identify what level of training and familiarisation will need to be given to people to enable them to perform effectively on Day 1.

The Mid-Transition Review Workshop is an ideal time for the Training and Familiarisation Coordinator to inform the Workshop attendees about the status of developing the Training and Familiarisation Plan. They should ensure that Workstream Leads are clear on what they need to deliver to enable the Plan to be completed.

Discuss topics that impact multiple Workstreams

At this point in the Transition, the Transition Management Team may have identified some cross-Workstream topics that need to be discussed. The Workshop provides a wonderful opportunity for all Workstream Leads to listen and participate in the discussions.

From a facilitation perspective, do try and identify these subjects ahead of the Workshop and allocate someone to present them. Good facilitation will be required if there are any particularly contentious issues being discussed, to keep the conversations focussed and to ensure that the Workshop agenda is not derailed. If there is any risk of these topics derailing the Workshop agenda, then it is advisable to schedule them after the Workshop has taken place.

4. Drive to Completion Phase

This Phase of the Transition commences after the Mid-Transition Review Workshop has been held. During this Phase, the Category A Deliverables are progressively closed out by the Workstream Leads and the focus turns to becoming operationally ready.

Category A Deliverables are Deliverables that must be completed prior to Completion taking place or are essential for the Transfer to take place on the designated date. Further information on categorisation of Deliverables can be found in the Programme Management section.

The Transition Management Team continue to monitor progress of the Transition Plan and how Transition Risks are reducing. As Completion Date draws nearer, the Team progressively looks for assurance from Workstream Leads that all Deliverables will be completed on time and that Risks will be mitigated or completed. The emphasis is on quickly surfacing issues and seeking to resolve them in an expedient manner.

During this Phase, it is common for the Workforce who are transferring to the new Owner to express a desire to get the deal done and start working in the new organisation. One of the things which can severely impact morale at this stage of the Transition is delaying Completion. Therefore, significant effort should be expended to keep closing out Deliverables and working towards transferring Operatorship at the planned date.

During this Phase, there are several pre-requisites to transferring Operatorship from Seller to Buyer:

- Hold an Operational Readiness Workshop.
- Resolve issues.
- Hold a Go/No-Go Decision Meeting, where the Steering Group formally confirm the intent to progress with the transfer, or not.
- Complete Assurance reviews.
- 'Sign-off'.
- Enact the Freeze Calendar and Cutover Plan.
- Ensure teams know what to do 'on the day'.

Each of these are broken down in more detail in this section of the book.

Hold an Operational Readiness Workshop

The purpose of the Operational Readiness Workshop is to get a clear understanding from Workstream Leads on their preparedness to sign-off their Category A Deliverables by Completion date. The Workshop is typically held one or two weeks before the Go/No-Go decision meeting. This gives Workstream Leads time to close out any actions arising from the Workshop before the Go/No-Go decision is taken.

You should expect the Steering Group, or people who have delegated authority from the Buyer and Seller companies, to attend the Workshop. If there are intractable issues that arise, then having the key decision makers from both companies in attendance can help get decisions made.

The Workshop has the following objectives:

1. Confirm how the Go/No-Go decision will be taken.

2. Review the status of the Sign-off Register and risks on the Risk Register, ensuring that there is clarity on what it will take to complete Deliverables and mitigate or complete risks.

3. Review the Transition Plan to ensure that affected personnel have adequate knowledge about systems and processes that will change.

4. Review the Applications and Infrastructure Freeze Calendar and Cutover Plan to ensure that they are comprehensive and provide sufficient clarity to everyone affected by them.

It is helpful to provide guidance to the Workstream Leads on how the Go/No-Go decision will be taken, who will be involved in making the decision, and when it will be taken.

You should ensure that you have answers ready to the following commonly asked questions:

- What happens if the decision is 'No-Go', which means that the Transition will not complete on the planned Completion Date? When would the new Completion Date be?
- The meeting to make a Go/No-Go decision is before all the Deliverables have been completed. What happens if one or two of the Deliverables that we expect to complete are not complete by Completion Date?

The bulk of the Workshop should be focussed on Workstream Leads providing an objective assessment of the status of their Workstream to the other Workshop attendees. The materials that they present should have been prepared beforehand, as pre-work.

Their assessment should cover the following topics:

- What is the status of their Sign-off Register? What Deliverables have been completed? What Deliverables have not yet been completed? What will it take to complete the outstanding Deliverables?
- What is the status of their Risk Register? What risks are still not mitigated or completed? What actions need to be taken to mitigate or complete them?
- What other issues do the Workstream Leads have that will impact their ability to complete?

You may find it helpful to outline your expectations of Workstream Leads during these status updates:

- To be as realistic and honest as possible. They need to articulate the status of their Workstream and their confidence in being ready for signing off their Deliverables. This Workshop is not a time to be defensive about what has or hasn't been done by the Workstream, but is an opportunity to give a cold, hard assessment of readiness.
- To identify what is standing in the way of completing and what is being done to address this. If problems are insurmountable, the Workstream Leads should be identifying what the 'Plan Bs' are and whether these are palatable.

From a facilitation perspective, the role of the other Workshop attendees is to test each Workstream's delivery status and 'yet to do' plan. So, the session should be designed to give the Workstream Leads time to give a high-level presentation of their status and at least as much time for questions and answers. Any areas of disagreement or issues that are raised, that cannot immediately be resolved, should be captured by the Facilitator. These should be reviewed with the Transition Management Team, to determine what actions need to be taken to resolve them.

The output of the Workshop is a list of critical outstanding actions that need to be completed for transition of Operatorship to occur safely and efficiently on Completion Date. Depending on the issues that arise during the Workshop, additional working sessions may be required, with a selection of Workstream Leads, to further discuss issues and agree action plans.

On one Transition that I was involved in, the timescale for completing the deal was very compressed. The Transition Management Team suspected that there were likely to be intractable issues that would need to be discussed with a selection of Workstream Leads. Therefore, we scheduled the Operational Readiness Workshop to take place over one and a half days. The first day was focussed on Workstream status updates and the second half day was used to bring the key Workstream Leads together to generate cross-Workstream action plans. To make best use of everyone's time, those Workstream Leads who were not required to participate in the second day's discussions were excused from participating.

Another focus area of the Operational Readiness Workshop should be to communicate the Freeze Calendar and Cutover Plan to all Workstream Leads. This session is usually led by the IT Workstream Leads, who present the detailed plans for cutting over Applications and Infrastructure.

Resolve Issues

During the Drive to Completion Phase, issues may emerge that have the potential to impact Completion Date. Commonly encountered issues relate to the following:

1. Issues with getting physical IT hardware installed and operational. For example, inability to run new cables to offices in the required timeframe, or problems with getting new hardware operational.

2. Issues with getting IT applications operational. User Acceptance Testing may not be completed within the required timeframe: particularly for complex systems that have taken a long time to build.

3. Commercial issues. This is quite commonplace in the Oil and Gas Industry. My experience is that Joint Venture Partners appear to hold out approving Transfer of Operatorship from the Seller to the Buyer until the last moment, until all their queries and disputes with the Seller have been resolved.

4. Contractual issues. Contracts between the Buyer and their Contractors have still not been finalised.

As issues emerge, it is helpful to apply the following framework to decide what type of resolution may be most appropriate to take. This is particularly relevant for those issues that have a high likelihood of significantly impacting the ability to complete the Transition on time.

1. Determine whether the issue can be resolved in accordance with the current Plan by Completion Date. If so, then continue to follow the Plan.

2. If the issue cannot be resolved in accordance with the current Plan, by Completion Date, then do the following:

   o Identify 'Plan Bs': workarounds that could be completed by Completion Date. If there are workable solutions, these should become the new 'Plan As' and the Workstream should prioritise completing them. Additional resources or money may need to be allocated to the Workstream, in which case the Transition Managers or Steering Group may need to approve these changes.
   o Determine how long after Completion Date the issue would take to resolve. The Buyer's team should assess what mitigations would need to be put in place to continue safely operating until the issue is resolved.
   o Determine whether a 'Transition Service Agreement' could be agreed between the Seller and Buyer. In some instances, the Seller may need to enter into a contractual arrangement with the Buyer to continue providing a limited number of services

after Completion Date, until sometime in the future.

o Consider escalating the issue within the Buyer and Seller's respective companies. This is particularly the case for commercial issues, which may need the assistance of the company's Board of Directors to resolve.

During the run up to Completion Date, the Programme Management rhythm may need to change. You should consider the following:

- Do you need to implement more frequent check-ins with Workstream Leads, to enable them to quickly raise issues or communicate completion of Deliverables?
- Do you need to schedule more frequent Steering Group meetings, to get decisions made quickly? This is particularly helpful if there were a lot of issues still outstanding at the time of the Go/No-Go Decision meeting.

Hold a Go/No-Go Decision Meeting

Prior to Completion Date, a critical decision needs to be made: whether to progress with Completion on the planned date or not. This decision needs to be formally taken by the Steering Group members at the Go/No-Go Decision meeting.

The timing of this meeting is important: it should be held before the Seller's Payroll team have instigated the process of issuing forms to staff to terminate their employment: P45's (UK term) or Pink Slip (US term). If a decision is taken after this point, then any deferral to Completion Date is likely to result in a very messy HR process and be distressful to staff, as P45's will have been issued.

There are several factors which need to be considered before a final decision is made:

1. Do you expect all the Category A Deliverables to be completed by the Decision date?

2. Are the Operational teams in a position that they can handover the operations in a safe way?

3. Will the Buyer be able to safely operate the assets immediately following Completion?

The Steering Group need to decide whether to:

1. Proceed with completion on the Planned Completion Date.

2. Change the date of the Planned Completion Date, usually deferring it to a later date.

3. Cancel the Transition.

It's very unlikely that the Steering Group members will decide to cancel the Transition at this meeting; this type of decision is normally related to changes in corporate objectives and is likely to be taken outside this meeting.

The Transition Management Team has a critical role to play in helping the Steering Group make a decision; they need to prepare and present a comprehensive overview of the state of the Transition to them. You should aim to prepare a Transition Decision Support Package containing the following, as a minimum:

1. Status of the Sign-off Register. Best practice is to present this as a heat map, enabling the Steering Committee to focus on which Deliverables haven't been completed.

2. Issues that have the biggest potential to impact the Go/No-Go Decision. The Transition Management Team should summarise what the issues are, their status and what activities need to be completed before Completion Date. It is helpful to get an indication from the Workstream Leads on their confidence in resolving the issues by Completion Date and what alternative options exist to allow Completion to proceed.

3. The status of Programme Management registers, such as the Risk Register and Transition Service Agreement Register.

4. The status of the Freeze Plan and Cutover Plan. It is particularly important to highlight any applications or infrastructure that is unlikely to be ready by Completion Date, and the risk that poses to safe operations.

5. Status of actions from the Operational Readiness Workshop that were agreed to be completed by the date of the Go/No-Go Decision meeting.

6. What the impact would be if the Steering Group decided to go ahead with the planned Completion Date and then later reversed the decision. You should aim to articulate the level of difficulty that would be required to respond to a change of date and its impact on company reputation and resources.

7. Depending on the timing of Completion Date, you may also need to assess such things as availability of people to support the cutover and Day 1 operations, particularly around holiday times.

Complete Assurance Reviews

As you can imagine, making the Go/No-Go decision is not a simple matter. To help inform the Steering Group, they may seek to get some external feedback. It is commonplace for the Buyer and/or Seller Steering Group members to ask an external party, who has previous experience of Transitions, to do some or all the following:

1. Independently meet with the Workstream Leads and test their readiness to complete all Category A Deliverables by Completion Date.

2. Participate in the Operational Readiness Workshop and provide external feedback on what they perceive to be the highest risks to being ready to complete on the planned Completion Date.

3. Conduct site visits to operational assets and test their readiness to operate the assets safely after Completion Date.

The review team should use their experience to identify and test areas where previous Transitions have had issues.

Once the Go or No-Go decision has been made, it is very important to quickly communicate the outcome to the Workstream Leads, so that they can take appropriate action.

'Sign-off'

One of the final requirements of the Drive to Completion Phase is to 'sign-off': to say that all Category A Deliverables have been completed and that the assets can be safely handed over to the Buyer. This is achieved by:

- Each Workstream Lead signing to confirm that all their Workstream's Category A Deliverables have been completed.
- The Transition Managers signing to confirm that all Transition Category A Deliverables have been completed.
- The Transition Managers, or someone else appointed by the Steering Group, signing to confirm that the assets can be safely handed over to the Buyer.

From a practical perspective, this sign-off should happen at least one day prior to the planned Completion Date. This gives the Transition Management Team time to secure all the relevant signatures.

If there are Category A Deliverables that cannot be signed off as complete, these should be escalated to the Steering Group for review. A decision will need to be taken whether to proceed with mitigations in place or defer Completion.

Once sign-off has been achieved, it authorises the lawyers to complete all the legal paperwork associated with the Sale and Purchase Agreement and any associated Agreements. It also authorises the Transition team to continue with Cutover: cutting the Seller's systems, processes and procedures over to the Buyer.

Enact the Freeze Calendar and Cutover Plan

The final stage of the Drive to Completion Phase is to enact the Freeze Calendar and Cutover Plan.

Early in this Phase, the IT Workstream should generate and publish a Freeze Calendar.

This Calendar gives a day by day visualisation of the period leading up to Completion Date when IT Applications will be:

- 'Frozen': Seller's Applications will not be available to existing users from this date. This is to enable the IT Workstream to extract data from the Application, ready to load it into the new Buyer's system.
- 'Loading': data from Seller's systems will be loaded into the Buyer's systems during this period.
- 'Live': Buyer's new Applications will be available from this date.

The IT Workstream will also generate and publish a Cutover Plan. This Plan is a very detailed step-by-step plan showing what needs to be done to power up the Buyer's infrastructure and applications, switch over (or cutover) the Seller's systems to the Buyer's systems, and then power down the Seller's systems.

Cutover typically involves the following steps:

- 'Freeze' the Seller Applications, as per the Freeze Calendar.
- Extract, redact and copy data from the Seller's Applications and transfer it to the Buyer via Chain of Custody processes.
- Load and synchronise data in the Buyer's system.
- Disable all Seller User accounts (access to Seller systems) and initiate cutover of networks from Seller to Buyer.
- Conduct final testing of Buyer systems, as per the agreed cutover sequence.
- Confirm Buyer IT systems are working.
- Seek business sign-off.
- 'Go-live' on a system-by-system basis.

- Enable user access to Buyer systems.

All Workstream Leads need to be familiar with the Cutover Plan. They should develop Business Continuity Plans, so that operations can continue during the period when the Seller's Applications are frozen and before the Buyer's Applications are live.

On the specified Completion Date, the Workstreams should complete their final planned activities. By this stage of the Transition, it is likely that the bulk of the workload will fall on the IT Workstreams. It is essential that they have sufficient people in place to complete the myriad of activities that will need to be undertaken.

During the Cutover period, the Transition Management Team should convene a daily meeting to:

1. Discuss progress of Cutover.

2. Highlight emerging issues and agree actions to resolve them.

Ensure Teams Know What to do 'On the Day'

A critical activity that must be undertaken in the Drive to Completion Phase is to ensure that everyone who will be impacted by the transfer of the assets are aware of how they will be impacted and what they need to do.

At its simplest, you need to identify:

- What is changing?
- Which people or teams will be impacted by the changes?
- What do they need to know and do?

Some of the communications you will need to make include:

- Informing people who use IT Applications and Infrastructure when these will be 'frozen' and not able to be used. They will also need to know what Business Continuity

Plans will be in place, enabling them to continue performing their role during this period.

- Giving information about when and where people will be expected to start work on Day 1, if the office that they work in is changing.
- Informing Contractors and Suppliers who they will need to send invoices to, for work that is conducted before, during and after Completion Date.

Workstream Leads have a crucial role in working with the people in their area of responsibility and ensuring that they are adequately prepared for Cutover.

5. Close Out Phase

This Phase commences once Cutover has been completed.

The key requirements of the Close Out Phase are to:

1. Complete all Category B Deliverables.

2. Implement Transition Service Agreements.

3. Conduct and publish a Lessons Learned Review.

4. Disband the Transition Teams.

This section of the book will elaborate on each of these points.

Complete all Category B Deliverables

During the Transition, it is likely that you will have identified Category B Deliverables; Deliverables that may be completed after Completion date. They fall into two categories:

1. Deliverables that are contingent on the Completion Date, such as Issuing the Final Completion Statement; decommissioning Seller IT infrastructure that was in use up until Completion Date; or, removing the asset from Seller systems.

2. Deliverables that were commenced but were not completed prior to Completion Date. An example of this is transferring archive hard copy documentation from Seller to Buyer.

The role of the Transition Management Team is to track these Category B Deliverables until completion.

Implement Transition Service Agreements

If there is a requirement for the Seller to provide Transition Service to the Buyer, for a period of time after Completion Date, these should be covered by a Transition Service Agreement. These are described in more detail in the Programme Management section.

The Seller's Transition Manager should ensure that a focal point is nominated for each Transition Service Agreement that is in place. The role of the focal point is to liaise with the Buyer, in the event of any questions or issues, and to monitor the Agreement until it is closed.

Conduct and Publish a Lessons Learned Review

It is best practice for each Workstream to hold a Lessons Learned Review shortly after Completion Date, whilst the lessons are still fresh in the Workstream Leads' memories.

The objective of this Review is to identify and capture specific examples of Best Practices and Lessons Learned. These should be consolidated and published to help future Transition Teams complete their work as efficiently as possible.

Disband the Transition Teams

It is uncommon for the Buyer and Seller companies to retain a standalone Transition Team for long. Instead, they take the outstanding Category B Deliverables and bring them back into their base organisation.

All documentation relating to the Transition should be consolidated and archived, for future reference. Any residual information not transferred to the Buyer for commercial or confidential reasons should be securely archived.

It is common for there to be questions from the Buyer in this Close Out Phase. Prior to disbanding, the Seller's Transition Manager should ensure that a focal point is nominated for responding to them.

Programme Management

To undertake a successful Transition, there is a requirement to establish and follow clear and simple Programme Management practices. The following practices have successfully been implemented on numerous Transitions throughout the Oil and Gas Industry. They are effective for both small and complex Transitions.

1. Transition Governance.

2. Transition Planning.

3. Transition Budgeting.

4. Risk Management.

5. Progress Reporting.

6. Document Collaboration.

7. Communications.

8. Programme Management Documents.

9. Transition Service Agreements.

This section of the book will provide further details on each of these Programme Management practices.

1. Transition Governance

Every successful Transition requires a simple governance structure to be in place. At its core, Transition Governance is concerned with steering the Transition to a successful outcome for both Seller and Buyer.

The following structure has proven to be effective in meeting these objectives:

- Establish a Steering Group, comprising of senior Executives from both the Seller and Buyer companies.
- Appoint two Transition Managers: one to lead the Seller's Workstream Leads and one to lead the Buyer's Workstream Leads.
- Appoint Workstream Leads who have the necessary experience to manage delivery of all their Workstream activities.

The roles of each of these parties is described in more detail below.

Role of the Steering Group

The Steering Group comprises of senior Executives from the Seller and Buyer's companies, supplemented by specialists as required.

Their role is to:

- Appoint the Transition Managers and hold them accountable for delivery.
- Delegate budget and resources to the Transition Managers to enable them to deliver the Transition within agreed constraints.
- Monitor progress of the Transition and ensure that it meets Seller and Buyer corporate goals.
- Monitor the achievement of Transition strategic objectives and consider any interventions to take.
- Provide oversight of 'red' risks (those on the Transition Risk Register in the High Probability – High Impact categories) and ensure that effective plans are in place to mitigate them.
- Make decisions that enable the Transition to proceed, especially where there is an impasse between Buyer and Seller Transition teams.

- Participate in Joint Steering Group meetings and Transition Workshops.
- Approve Transition Service Agreements.
- Determine what level of independent assurance needs to be undertaken during the Transition and appoint reviewers to perform the review.
- Formally make the Go/No-Go decision: to progress with Completion on the planned date or not.

Role of the Transition Managers

The role of the Transition Manager is to manage the Workstream Leads and successfully deliver the Transition.

Their role is to:

- Appoint Workstream Leads and the Transition Management Team and hold them accountable for delivery.
- Provide overall management of the Workstream Leads and Workstreams.
- Prepare a Transition Plan that identifies all activities and milestones that are required to be completed to successfully transition the assets from Seller to Buyer. Monitor progress and intervene when required.
- Prepare a Transition Budget that aligns with the Transition Plan and which identifies all costs associated with completing the Transition. Manage delivery of costs within the agreed budget.
- Implement comprehensive Programme Management practices (including Transition Planning, Transition Budgeting, Risk Management, Progress Reporting, Document Collaboration, Communications, Programme Management Documents, and Transition Service Agreements).
- Sign-off to confirm that all Transition Deliverables have been completed.
- If requested by the Steering Group, sign-off to confirm that the assets can be safely handed over to the Buyer.

Role of Workstream Leads

The role of a Workstream Lead is to transition all the defined scope within their area of responsibility, from Seller to Buyer, within the specified timeline. For the duration of the Transition, the Workstream Leads report to the Transition Manager for all their Workstream-related work.

Their role is to:

- Prepare a Workstream Plan that identifies all activities and milestones that are required to be completed to successfully transition all the defined scope within the Workstream's area of responsibility from Seller to Buyer. Monitor progress and intervene when required.
- Identify and secure people and resources to deliver the Workstream Plan.
- Prepare a Workstream Budget that aligns with the Plan and which identifies all Workstream costs associated with completing the Transition. Manage delivery of costs within the agreed budget.
- Engage, monitor and supervise Workstream members to complete all Workstream activities in a timely manner.
- Provide support to other Workstreams to ensure delivery of cross-Workstream deliverables.
- Fulfil all Programme Management requirements (including updating plans, reports and risks registers; and attending meetings and workshops).
- Sign-off to confirm that each Workstream Deliverable has been completed.

Joint Governance meetings

Throughout the Transition, the following governance meetings will take place:

- Joint Steering Group meeting.
- Joint Transition Management Team meeting.
- Joint Transition Team meeting.

Each of these are described in more detail below.

Joint Steering Group meeting

Joint Steering Group meetings enable the Steering Group to monitor progress of the Transition and steer it towards a successful conclusion.

The purpose of the meeting is to review progress, provide oversight of 'red' risks, ratify the plan, and deal with issues that have been raised by the Transition Managers.

I have found these meetings to be most effective when there are open and frank discussions between all attendees. To enable these types of conversations to occur, the style of the meeting is important. They should not be 'death by PowerPoint', where there are numerous slides giving commentary on every aspect of the Transition. Rather, they should be focussed around critical topics.

A typical agenda will be:

1. Transition Decisions. The Transition Managers discuss what decisions require Steering Group input before they can be made. Depending on the decision that is being discussed, decisions can be made during the meeting and recorded on a Decision Register or actions recorded on an Action Log to enable the decision to be made at a future date.

2. Support Required. The Transition Managers discuss what support they need from the Steering Group.

3. Transition Status. All this information should be issued in advance of the meeting, as pre-read, therefore this section of the meeting should be by exception only. The Steering Group agree what interventions need to be taken to get performance back on track. Topics include:

   o Progress against strategic objectives.
   o Plan status.
   o Progress towards mitigating Transition risks.
   o Transition cost estimate versus budget.
   o Key achievements since last meeting.

4. Any Other Business.

5. Review and agree Decisions Made and Actions.

Joint Steering Group meetings are typically held monthly, although you may choose to hold them every two weeks in periods of high activity, especially towards the end of the Transition.

It is desirable to hold this meeting soon after the Joint Transition Management Team meeting, so that any issues that have been reported that require Steering Group intervention can be dealt with in a timely manner.

Joint Transition Management Team meeting

Throughout the Transition, the Buyer's and Seller's Transition Management Teams need to work collaboratively with each other. This will be achieved through ongoing conversations. However, a formal Joint Transition Management Team meeting will be held on a regular basis to discuss progress and intervene where required.

A typical agenda will be:

- Resolution of Issues.
- Transition Plan look ahead.
- Interventions that need to be taken.
- Agreement on agenda and contents of upcoming Workshops (as required).

- Agreement on agenda and contents of upcoming Joint Steering Group meetings (as required).
- Review of agreed Specific, Measurable and Time-bound Actions.

Joint Transition Management Team meetings are typically held weekly.

Joint Transition Team meeting

The focus of the meeting is on sharing context and direction from the Transition Management Team and highlighting and discussing cross-Workstream issues that need to be resolved.

All members of the Buyer's and Seller's Transition Management Teams and all Workstream Leads attend this meeting. The meeting is held shortly after the consolidated Transition Progress Report has been issued, and the expectation is that Workstream Leads will have read the report.

A typical agenda will be:

- Context from Transition Managers.
- Feedback from each Workstream on issues and concerns that have arisen, or anything that is holding the Workstream back from progressing.
- Review of agreed Specific, Measurable and Time-bound Actions.

Workstream Leads are not expected to provide a detailed progress update during the meeting. These are captured in the Joint Progress Report. Workstream contributions should focus on matters that affect the Transition as a whole, or other Workstreams.

Joint Transition Team meetings are typically held every two weeks.

2. Transition Planning

Transition Planning is the process of creating a high quality, fully integrated Transition Plan from well-defined, individual activities at Workstream level and then managing changes to the Plan.

Generating a Transition Plan is essential, for the following reasons:

- It provides your Workstream Leads with a structured Plan to follow. This enables them to keep their focus on delivering the myriad activities they will need to finish before Completion Date. It also helps them to complete tasks at the right time and in the right order.
- It enables you to generate a High Level Strategic Plan for the Transition. I have found this to be an important document that can be used to communicate progress of the Transition to the Workforce, Workstream Leads and the Steering Group.
- It helps ensure that cross-Workstream activities are identified and appropriately resourced.
- It provides a tangible basis for assessing how the Transition is progressing.

The best approach to creating a fully-integrated Transition Plan is to complete the following steps:

- Step 1. Identify Workstream Scopes of Work.
- Step 2. Identify Deliverables for each Scope of Work.
- Step 3. Categorise Deliverables as Category A or B.
- Step 4. Identify Activities that need to be completed.
- Step 5. Create the Transition Plan.
- Step 6. Identify Interdependencies.
- Step 7. Use the Plan to manage Transition delivery.

Each of these steps will now be described in more detail below.

Step 1. Identify Workstream Scopes of Work.

The Scopes of Work are the big categories or 'buckets' of work that will need to be completed by a Workstream. The Scopes of Work do not have to be well defined or time-bound; they are purely to help the Workstream Leads identify all the work they need to do, at a high level.

Some examples are given below for five key Workstreams. These examples are meant to be illustrative only and are taken from the UK Oil and Gas Industry.

Scopes of Work for People Workstream:

1. Employee Consultation.

2. Transfer of Employer's Liability Information (data that Seller must pass on to Buyer about the employees who are being transferred).

3. Establishment of Buyer Organisation.

4. Recruitment.

5. HR Infrastructure of Buying Company (including Pay, Grading, Bonuses, Pension, Benefits).

6. Employee Induction Plan.

Scopes of Work for IT Workstream:

1. IT Infrastructure.

2. IT Applications.

3. Digital Data handover.

4. Freeze Calendar and Cutover Plan.

Scopes of Work for Safety, Health & Environment Workstream:

1. Licence to Operate – Safety Case/Pipelines/Onshore Facilities.

2. PLANC – Permits, Licences, Authorisations, Notifications and Consents.

3. Engagement with Safety, Health and Environmental stakeholders and Industry Bodies.

4. Emergency Response and Incident Management.

5. Occupational Health and Industrial Hygiene.

6. Security.

Scopes of Work for Finance & Tax Workstream

1. Sale and Purchase Agreement requirements (including interim and final completion statements).

2. Financial systems and processes.

3. Budget and cost management.

4. Tax requirements.

5. Hydrocarbon accounting.

6. Insurance.

Scopes of Work for Logistics & Procurement Workstreams

1. Logistics strategy and processes.

2. Transferring Seller Contract information.

3. Setting up Buyer Contracts (including Contract Strategy, Novations, Negotiations).

4. Inventory.

Step 2. Identify Deliverables for each Scope of Work

The second step is to break down the Scopes of Work and identify the associated Deliverables that need to be completed during the Transition. Once identified, they will be categorised as either Category A or B Deliverables. The Category A Deliverables are those that Workstream leads will sign-off at the end of the Transition.

Some examples of Deliverables are shown below for the People Workstream. You will see the linkage to the Scopes of Work that have previously been identified.

Scope of Work	Deliverables
Employee Consultation.	1. Nomination, Election and training of Employee Representatives completed. 2. Consultation meetings completed. 3. Final Measures confirmed, and Consultation process closed.
Transfer of Employer's Liability Information.	1. Letters sent to transferring Employees identifying what data will be shared. 2. All data provided to Buyer in accordance with statutory requirements.
Establishment of Buyer Organisation.	1. Organisational design approved. 2. Organisational design issued.
Recruitment.	1. All new and vacant positions identified. 2. Resourcing strategy finalised.
HR Infrastructure of Buying Company.	1. Pay and grading structure defined. 2. Bonus and Benefits defined. 3. Benefit scheme contracts placed. 4. Pension scheme provider selected.
Employee Induction Plan.	1. Employee Induction Plan developed and ready to implement.

Step 3. Categorise Deliverables as Category A or B

It is customary practice for the Sale and Purchase Agreement and Transfer of Operatorship Agreement to divide Deliverables into two categories: usually Category A or Category B Deliverables.

Category A Deliverables are Deliverables that must be completed prior to Completion taking place or are essential for the Transfer to take place on the designated date.

Category B Deliverables are Deliverables that may be completed after Completion date.

From a practical perspective, it is helpful to ensure that both Transition Management Teams and all Workstream Leads have a shared understanding of what Category A and Category B Deliverables are. A test I commonly use to determine whether a Deliverable should be categorised as A or B is to ask the question: "If this Deliverable doesn't get completed, will it stop the Transition from taking place?" If the answer is "Yes", then it is a Category A Deliverable.

Here are some examples:

Deliverable	Implication if it is not completed by Completion Date	Conclusion
Employee 'TUPE' Consultation Meetings and Consultation Process Completed.	This is a legislative requirement, if people are being transferred from one company to another.	This is a Category A Deliverable. If it does not get completed the Transfer cannot proceed.
Safety Case has been accepted by the Health and Safety Executive.	This is commonly a Condition Precedent of the deal.	This is a Category A Deliverable. If it does not get accepted, the Transfer cannot proceed.
Emergency Response Structure and Process tested and in place.	The Buyer's team may not be able to respond to an incident on the assets being transferred, leading to loss of life and potential prosecution.	This is a Category A Deliverable. If it does not get completed, the Transfer cannot proceed.
Replace all Seller-branded signage on the assets with Buyer signage.	In the event of an incident, media may publish photographs of the asset with incorrect signage.	This is a Category B Deliverable. Signage is replaced once the deal has completed and there is no longer any risk of the Transition being delayed or stopped.
Final Completion Statement reviewed and agreed by both Parties.	The Final Completion Statement can only be completed after Completion Date.	This is a Category B Deliverable.

One of the common errors that I have seen is for Workstream Leads to confuse categorisation of Deliverables into As and Bs with the importance of the Deliverables. It is perfectly acceptable to have Category B Deliverables that are very important to deliver in advance of Completion Date. However, you should avoid the temptation to turn these into Category A Deliverables.

An example of this would be the requirement for the Finance team to issue the Final Completion Statement; the final reconciliation of the Sales price, including such things as working capital adjustments. Issuing the Final Completion Statement is a very important, high priority activity to both Buyer and Seller. However, it is not a Category A activity. This activity can only take place after Completion Date, therefore, it is a Category B Deliverable.

You should ensure that your Workstream Leads are clear on the differences between these two concepts.

It is tempting for Transition teams to break down all their Deliverables into activities and categorise them as either Category A or B activities. From my experience, it is best to keep the categorisation of As and Bs at the Deliverables level and not try to assign them to Activities. This enables you to 'see the wood from the trees'.

As Workstream Leads develop their list of Deliverables, check that they are Specific, Measurable and Action-Oriented. This will help them to sign-off the Deliverables at the end of the Transition.

Step 4. Identify Activities that Need to be Completed

The fourth step is to identify all the activities that need to be undertaken to deliver each of the Deliverables. These activities need to be Specific, Measurable and Action-Oriented. The activities also need to be time-bound:

- Identify start and end dates of activities that will take time to complete; or

- Identify the date an activity will be started or ended. This type of activity is called a milestone.

Do ensure that each Workstream Lead fully identifies their Scopes of Work and Deliverables before starting to identify the associated activities. I cannot emphasise enough the importance of doing this.

Continuing with the People Workstream, the table below shows how Deliverables in the Employee Consultation Scope of Work have been broken down into detailed activities. Start and end dates and Milestones have been identified.

Deliverable	Activities
Nomination, Election and training of Employee Representatives completed.	1. Nominate Employee Representatives: 1 July to 21 July. 2. Conduct training for Management Representatives: 25 July. 3. Conduct training for Employee Representatives: 28 July.
Consultation meetings completed.	1. Prepare and conduct Consultation Meeting 1: 1 – 7 August. 2. Prepare and conduct Consultation Meeting 2: 8 – 14 August. 3. Prepare and conduct Consultation Meeting 3: 15 – 21 August.
Final Measures confirmed, and Consultation process closed.	1. Final measures confirmed, and consultation process completed: 21 August.

Step 5. Create the Transition Plan

The fifth step of Transition Planning is for the Transition Planner to create the Transition Plan. All the Workstream activities are entered into a Planning software package, such as Microsoft Project or Primavera, by the Transition Planner. The Planning tool integrates all the individual Workstream-level activities together to produce one overall Plan in a variety of formats. These can be printed or shared with Workstream Leads, as required.

To enable you to generate and maintain a high-quality Plan, you need to consider the following key factors:

1. Employ a high-quality Transition Planner. From my experience, you want someone who is competent with using the Planning software and who can manage an atypical project Plan. It is equally important to employ someone who can interact well with Workstream Leads. It is a surety that some of your Workstream Leads will be unfamiliar with the practicalities of Planning, therefore it is very important that the Transition Planner has the interpersonal skills to provide them with ongoing training and support.

2. Select the best Planning software for the Transition. Although the choice of Planning software that is used will not make or break the Transition Plan, my experience is that it is better to use Primavera rather than Microsoft Project. In my opinion, Primavera is better equipped to create layouts that are visually appealing to the user and that progresses activities in a more meaningful way.

Step 6. Identify Interdependencies

The sixth step involves identifying interdependencies between Workstreams.

Interdependencies are defined as activities or deliverables that are dependent on more than one Workstream for their delivery. An example is developing the Buyer organisation. In this example, the People Workstream will most likely coordinate the development of the new organisation. However, it will require input from each of the Workstreams to ensure that their business processes can be supported. If one of the Workstreams fails to provide information to the People Workstream at the required time, the overall organisational structure will be compromised.

One of the best ways of establishing interdependencies is for the Workstream Leads to review each other's Plans and identify where they need support from each other. A tried and tested way of enabling these conversations to take place is to hold an interactive Plan Review Workshop. At this event, the Workstream Leads can walk around a room and interact with other Workstream Leads whilst looking at each other's Plans.

Once interdependencies have been identified, the Transition Planner should build them into the overall Transition Plan. This makes the linkage between Workstream activities transparent. It gives Workstream Leads clarity on when they need to complete activities that support the delivery of another Workstream's activities or Deliverables.

Step 7. Use the Plan to manage Transition delivery

Once a fully integrated Transition Plan has been created, it provides the basis for managing delivery of the Transition. The Plan provides the Transition Management Team with:

- Visibility about what each Workstream is working on.
- How Workstreams are progressing: are they completing their activities in a timely manner or not? If delays start to materialise, the Transition Management Team can intervene to prevent major milestones or Deliverables being missed.

To enable the Plan to be used as a performance management tool, it is essential that the Workstream Leads accurately report their progress on a regular basis.

I have found the following ingredients to be necessary to create a high-quality Plan:

1. Your Transition Planner should implement a simple to follow process that enables Workstream Leads to quickly update actual and forecast start and finish dates.

2. Spend time educating the Workstream Leads on the importance of the Transition Plan and how to provide the required updates to the Transition Planner.

3. Consistently ask for plan updates from Workstream Leads. I have found that if you issue Plans and ask for updates from Workstream Leads on a consistent frequency (for example, two-weekly), the quality of the Plan updates that you receive will be high. Conversely, if your Transition Planner is inconsistent in asking for updates, you will find the quality of the updates is poor.

4. Ensure that your Workstream Leads know that you value the Transition Plan and regularly review it. I recommend that the Transition Management Team review all Plans after they have been updated by the Transition Planner. Follow up with Workstream Leads on any key dates that have changed.

5. Solicit feedback from the Transition Planner on how the plan quality could be improved and provide this feedback at Joint Transition Team meetings and Workshops.

Following each Plan update cycle, the Transition Planner should publish a set of standard reports. The following list gives an indication of commonly used reports:

1. High Level Strategic Plan – this report is a high-level, visual summary of the critical milestones and Deliverables through the life cycle of the Transition. It shows which ones have been completed, and if any have slipped. It is commonly used by the Steering Group to review progress of the Transition. It is also a very useful vehicle for communicating progress of the Transition to internal and external parties.

2. Deliverable Run-Down Curve – this report has two lines: the first one shows the target profile of Deliverable completion; the second shows the actual profile of Deliverable completion. By comparing the two lines, you

can see whether Deliverable completion is ahead or behind schedule.

3. Transition Plan – this report is a compilation of all Workstream Plans. It is typically produced in a Gantt chart format.

4. Workstream Plans – these reports are specific to an individual Workstream and are typically produced in a Gantt chart format. They are used by Workstream Leads and their teams to help them identify what activities need to be worked on next.

5. Transition S-Curve – this report shows how cumulative costs or labour hours are trending against a baseline target. The report has two lines: the first one is the baseline Transition S-Curve, which is flatter at the beginning and end and steeper in the middle. This is typical of most Transitions. The second line represents actual progress. However, S-Curves require resource-loaded plans to be in place and Transition Plans typically do not have resources loaded into them. For this reason, any S-Curves that are produced by the Transition Planner will be a 'fudge' – they are useful for giving general direction but are not absolutely accurate.

3. Transition Budgeting

Within the UK Continental Shelf, Transfer of Operatorship is recognised as a valid Joint Venture activity by most, if not all, Joint Operating Agreements. All the costs associated with Transition are charged to the Joint Venture accounts and allocated to the Partners in proportion to their equity share.

The overall Transition Budget is made up of the Seller Transition Budget and the Buyer Transition Budget. The team negotiating the Sale and Purchase Agreement will generate a 'top-down' Transition Budget, building on their experience from previous Transitions.

The 'bottoms-up' budgeting process commences in the Kick-Off Workshop, when the Workstream Leads are asked to provide an initial estimate of Workstream resources and costs. This cost estimate forms part of the Terms of Reference for the Workstream. Following this initial review, it is advisable for Workstream Leads to sit down with the person leading the development of the Company's Transition Budget and develop a more comprehensive estimate.

For the majority of Workstreams, their Budget is likely to comprise of mostly manpower and Travel & Expense (T&E) costs, as well as contracted support to assist in the completion of Workstream activities.

The table below provides an overview of other expenditures that you may see being incurred.

Workstream	Seller Non-Manpower/ T&E Costs	Buyer Non-Manpower/Travel & Expense (T&E) Costs
Safety, Health & Environment.		Cost of permit transfers; Support to write Safety Case; Emergency response provision; Emergency response exercises and training; Regulatory charges; Radiation permits and licences; Permitting/license approval.
IT.	Additional cabling and power.	Software licenses; Hardware; Cabling and circuits; Third party charges (for example Security penetration testing); Service fees (for example Cloud storage; managed servers).
Document Management.		Data storage facility costs.
Transition Management Team.	Workshop costs.	Branding and signage; Marketing materials; Workshop costs.
Operations.		Personal Protective Equipment.

By the time of the Plan Review Workshop, you should be able to generate a robust 'bottoms-up' Transition Budget. This will be presented to the Steering Group for approval.

Normal practice is to provide a monthly forecast of expenditure versus budget at the Steering Group meeting.

Some practical tips:

1. Do set up Transition Cost Codes as soon as the deal has been announced. Your IT Workstream is likely to want to start conducting discovery work as soon as possible. Likewise, your Safety, Health & Environment Workstream may need to set up contracts to enable them to start progressing Safety Case work.

2. Do set up individual Cost Codes for each Workstream. This enables the Workstream Leads to easily track their commitments and expenditures and facilitates the monthly update process.

3. Ensure that all Workstream Leads are clear on what can and cannot be included in the Transition Budget. This is especially important as Joint Venture Partners are likely to audit the costs at a future date.

4. Care should be taken to ensure that Transaction costs (those relating to marketing the asset and subsequent negotiation costs) are not incorporated into the Transition budget.

5. Ensure that Workstreams do not build in Unallocated Provision into their Workstream Budgets. If Unallocated Provision is required, this should be held at the Transition Management Team level.

4. Risk Management

An essential element of Programme Management is to ensure that all risks to delivering a successful Transition are identified and that sufficient actions are in place to mitigate or eliminate them. This can be achieved by implementing the following four steps:

1. Generate individual Workstream Risk Registers.

2. Ensure consistency between Risk Registers.

3. Ensure appropriate risk mitigation actions are in place.

4. Manage the Risk Management process.

The remainder of this section will elaborate on each of these points.

1. Generate Individual Workstream Risk Registers

Workstream Risk Registers can be generated at any point in the Transition, however it has proven most effective for Workstream Leads to generate them during the Plan Review Workshop.

At this time, they should have clarity on all the Workstream activities that they will be undertaking, in support of completing the defined Deliverables. They will most likely have a good appreciation of the risks that will prevent the Deliverables from being completed.

The best practice from previous Transitions is to keep Risk Registers as simple as possible. They comprise the following elements:

1. A description of the Risk.

2. The Consequence or Credible outcome if the risk materialises.

3. The Probability of the Risk occurring. To keep it simple, you should only have three levels of probability that Workstream Leads assess the Risk against. The most common levels that are used for Transitions are Low, Medium and High; however, other levels can be used, such as Rare, Possible and Almost Certain. Avoid the temptation

to use four or more levels; it creates unnecessary complexity and gives the impression that you have more precise information on the probability levels than is likely to be the case.

4. The Impact of the Risk occurring. The best practice from previous successful Transitions is to have three levels of impact:

   o High impact: Will stop the Transition from occurring or will delay it from occurring on the scheduled Completion date.
   o Medium impact: Will cause major disruption to the Transition but will not stop it from occurring, or cause it to be delayed beyond the scheduled Completion date.
   o Low impact: Will cause a minor disruption to the Transition.

5. A list of mitigating actions that need to be taken to reduce the probability of the risk occurring or to reduce the severity of the impact.

6. The Risk Owner. This is the person accountable for ensuring that the mitigating actions are being progressed in a timely manner.

7. Other elements that are used to manage the Risk Register, including Actionee, Current Status and any Commentary on the risks.

Once the risks have been evaluated they can be plotted on a Boston Square, which helps visually identify risks in the High Probability – High Impact category and other categories.

Writing down a superior quality description of the risk is required to generate meaningful mitigations. To ensure that your Workstream Leads generate superior quality risk descriptions, they should be encouraged to write risks that describe what might happen and why.

Some examples of good risk descriptions are:

- The Joint Venture Partners do not approve the Transfer of Operatorship, claiming Buyer is not technically and financially competent.
- Category A contracts are not in place by Completion Date, preventing procurement of critical materials or services, due to lack of people within the Procurement Workstream.

In both examples, you will see that the risk description describes what might happen and why.

Conversely, here are some examples of bad risk descriptions:

- Safety Case approval.
- Loss of key people.

Better wordings might be:

- Health and Safety Executive do not accept the Safety Case by scheduled Completion Date due to it being submitted late, as a result of not having dedicated people to write it.
- There are resignations of asset personnel in safety critical positions because they have not been kept sufficiently informed of the Transition process.

A similar approach to this needs to be taken to ensure that Workstream Leads provide good descriptions of consequences or credible outcomes if the risk materialises.

2. Ensure Consistency between Risk Registers

Once the Workstream Risk Registers have been created, there is a requirement to compare all Risk Registers and ensure that there is consistency in how individual Workstreams have each chosen to score the Impact of the Risk and the Probability of it occurring.

The best practice to ensure consistency across Workstreams is to arrange cross-Workstream reviews of risk registers, once the risk registers have all been populated.

I have found that you can have very effective conversations if you bring together three or four similar Workstreams (for example, Operations, Maintenance and Engineering Workstreams). The purpose of the meeting is to share risks and to calibrate how each Workstream has scored them.

The Transition Management Team typically facilitate these meetings and ensure that any learnings are transferred to other groups of Workstreams when they meet.

3. Ensure that Risk Mitigation Actions are in Place

Once each risk has been clearly articulated, the next step is to identify specific actions that can be taken to minimise or eliminate the risks. Risk mitigation actions can be directed towards reducing the severity of risk consequence or reducing the probability of the risk materialising.

From a Transition Management Team perspective, it is important to ensure that the Workstream Leads identify Specific, Measurable and Time-bound mitigating actions. It is also helpful to record whether the risk will be eliminated if all the actions are completed, or whether the risk will still be present but reduced to an acceptable level of impact or probability of occurrence.

4. Manage the Risk Management Process

After having created the Workstream Risk Registers, it is important that these are kept up to date by the Workstream Leads. The best practice is to require them to be updated at the same time as Workstream Plans are updated and Transition Progress Reports are written.

The position of the risk on the Boston Square will determine what level of oversight of the risks is undertaken. The purpose of this oversight is to gain assurance that the mitigating actions will reduce the risk to an acceptable level, and to ensure that risk mitigating actions are being completed in a timely manner.

Best practice is for the following levels of oversight:

- For 'Red' risks on the Boston Square: oversight is provided by the Steering Group.
- For 'Amber' risks: oversight is provided by the Transition Management Team.
- For 'Green' risks: oversight is provided by the relevant Workstream Lead.

It is customary for the status and progress on mitigating 'Red' risks to be reviewed at Steering Group meetings, enabling the Steering Group to discharge their accountability for overseeing them.

5. Progress Reporting

Throughout the Transition, it is essential to keep a close eye on progress. Depending on the progress that is being reported, you may need to intervene and initiate actions to get progress back on track.

There are two distinct types of progress reporting: Joint Progress reporting and Company Specific Progress reporting. This section of the book will elaborate on both types of reporting.

Joint Progress Reporting

It is customary to produce a formal written report of progress on a regular basis: the Transition Progress Report. For most Transitions, a two-weekly reporting cycle is sufficient. The report provides an update on:

- Key Workstream activities that have been completed since the last report was written.
- Cross-workstream or significant issues that the Workstream Leads need help to resolve.
- Major milestones or activities that Workstream Leads envisage completing in the next reporting cycle.

Each of the Workstreams write their own individual report and these are consolidated into the overall Transition Progress Report. This can be shared with the Workstream Leads and the Steering Group, enabling them to get a useful overview of progress.

It is important that these reports are as focused as possible, conveying all the required information. Workstream Leads should be discouraged from generating lengthy updates.

Progress is discussed at the following Joint meetings:

1. Joint Steering Group meeting – this meeting enables the Steering Group to monitor progress of the Transition and steer it towards a successful conclusion. It is attended by the Steering Group and Transition Managers.

2. Joint Transition Management Team meeting – this meeting provides a formal opportunity for the Buyers and Sellers Transition Management Teams to discuss progress and intervene where required.

3. Joint Transition Team Meeting – the focus of this meeting is on sharing context and direction from the Transition Management Team and highlighting and discussing cross-Workstream issues that need to be resolved. All members of the Buyers and Sellers Transition Management Teams and all Workstream Leads attend this meeting.

For more detailed information on the content of these meetings, see the section on Joint Governance Meetings.

Company Specific Progress Reporting

The Buyer and Seller Companies usually require internal meetings to be set up to discuss progress. These meetings provide the team with an opportunity to discuss internal blockers to progress and to highlight and discuss issues that may emerge between Buyer and Seller. The following meetings are typically held:

1. Workstream Lead Progress Review Meeting – the Transition Management Team and the Workstream Leads attend this meeting. The focus of the meeting is on providing support to the Workstream Leads to deliver their Plan; to review Workstream progress and identify any interventions that need to be taken; to discuss issues and how to resolve them; and to inform the Workstream Leads of any additional context from a company perspective. These meetings can take several forms, each of which are effective:

   o One-to-one check-ins with Individual Workstream Leads.
   o Groups of Workstream Leads together.
   o All the Workstream Leads together.

   My bias is to have one-to-one check-ins with critical Workstream Leads (those that have lots of activities, or where their activities are on the critical path – such as IT Workstream and Safety, Health & Environment Workstream) and then divide the remaining Workstream Leads into groups of similar Workstreams (such as Operations, Engineering and Maintenance).

2. Briefing Steering Group member – the Transition Manager should maintain a close relationship with their Steering Group member and brief them on:

   o Any emerging issues that will require resolution at the Steering Group level.
   o Any discussion points that are likely to arise at the Joint Steering Group Meeting.

o   Any areas where Workstream Leads are falling behind Plan that need support or intervention from the Steering Group member to resolve.

6. Document Collaboration

Throughout the course of the Transition, there will be a requirement for the Buyer and Seller Transition Teams to share documents with one another. The types of documents that are likely to be shared include:

- Terms of Reference documents.
- Transition Plans.
- Risk Registers.
- Transition Progress reports.
- Workshop materials.
- Workstream-specific materials that Workstream Leads wish to share with one another.

To facilitate sharing of documents, you should set up a secure document collaboration space that all Workstream Leads have access to.

Note that sharing documents for collaborative purposes is not the same as the formal process of transferring data and documents from Seller to Buyer. The Document Management and IT Workstreams are instrumental in establishing robust chain of custody processes to transfer the hundreds of thousands or millions of documents securely. They will also ensure that transfer of personal information is conducted in accordance with statutory obligations.

7. Communications

The role of Communications throughout the Transition cannot be underestimated. Many companies choose to include a Communications Specialist in their Transition Management Team, to help them engage their internal and external stakeholders.

Communications commence in the Pre-announcement Preparation Phase, with the creation of the Stakeholder Communication Plan. The intent of this Plan is to manage the announcement of the Sale and Purchase Agreement to the company's internal and external stakeholders.

Communications continue throughout the Transition with the objective of:

- Keeping internal stakeholders informed about progress of the Transition.
- Giving information about how to prepare for the upcoming transfer to agency personnel, contractors and 'ring-fenced' employees (those people in the Seller's company that will be transferring to the Buyer).
- Informing media sources at key points during the Transition and responding to media queries.

Employee Communications

There is a real danger that, if you fail to communicate well with the people most affected by the Sale and Purchase, particularly employees, you will see an increase in the symptoms of stress, as well as increased levels of employee attrition.

The following communication channels are tried and tested ways to keep employees informed of progress and give them opportunities to ask questions and get responses to them.

1. Establishment of an internal website. Websites allow the Transition Management Team to post materials that people can read at their leisure. Web-forms can be created to enable people to ask questions about the Transition. These are directed to relevant members of the Transition team to answer. The answers are then posted back on the website. Building up a repository of searchable Questions and Answers helps cut down on the requirement for the Transition Management Team to keep answering the same question.

2. Publishing a regular newsletter to impacted Employees. The newsletter should provide updates on Transition progress and keep everyone informed of future Plans. Best practice is to ask each of the Workstream Leads to contribute towards the development of the newsletter.

3. Posters, Brochures and Handouts. Posters and Brochures can be prepared and made available in the workspaces where the affected people work. They can cover such topics as: Who is the Buying Company? Key dates for Diaries. Key news from the Buyer's company. The Buyer may wish to hand out stationary or other office supplies, branded with their company's logo.

4. Face-to-Face 'Townhall meetings'. Holding regular Townhall meetings with employees is very effective. These meetings provide the opportunity for employees to collectively hear about progress and get answers to questions. Whoever is leading the meeting should ensure that they are familiar with the status of the Transition, and also understand what issues and questions are likely to be raised during the meeting.

Agency and Contract Worker Communications

Due to Employment Law requirements, the Buyer and Seller will not want to communicate any contractual information to affected Contractor's, instead leaving the Agency or Service Provider to determine the appropriate level of communication with their personnel.

However, I have found it beneficial to communicate general, non-contractual, Transition information to the Contractor community.

The following approaches can be taken to give Contractors context throughout the Transition:

- Issue general information on how the Transition is progressing through a newsletter or website.

- Incorporate general information on Transition progress into existing briefings given to contractors, such as Welcome Briefs when personnel land on an offshore installation for the start of their trip.
- Produce Information posters on Transition progress and display these on notice boards in public areas.
- Brief Contractor Managers on Transition progress any time they are gathered together, for example at Quarterly Safety Meetings.

Communications should state that Contractors and Agency personnel should contact their own employers with questions about contracts or terms and conditions.

Partner Communications

In the Oil and Gas Industry, it is common for assets to be owned by multiple Joint Venture Partners. Early and ongoing engagement with the Partners is essential.

Joint Operating Agreements or Licence Agreements may have 'pre-emption' clauses in them, where the Joint Venture Partners have an option to buy some or all the assets for the same consideration as agreed by the Buyer in the Sale and Purchase Agreement.

Once the pre-emption window has closed, the Joint Venture Partners may still have a role in approving the Buyer as successor Operator under the relevant Licences and Operating Agreements.

It has proven to be helpful to establish a series of regularly occurring meetings involving representatives from the Buyer, Seller and Joint Venture Partner companies throughout the period of the Transition. In the early days of these meetings, they are likely to be led by representatives from the Seller company, as they have an existing relationship with the Partners. As the Transition progresses, the leadership naturally changes to the Buyer.

Topics for discussion should include:

- Introduction of the Buyer to the Partners.
- Status of the Transition.
- Commercial issues. The Joint Venture Partners typically have a list of 'demands' that they want to resolve prior to completion of the deal. Each of these needs to be identified, discussed and resolved.
- Technical issues. The Joint Venture Partners may have technical questions for the Buyer that need to be discussed and resolved.

8. Programme Management Documents

To facilitate the smooth Transition of assets from Seller to Buyer, there are four sets of critical Programme Management documentation that should be agreed and written down.

1. How the Transition will be Governed document.

2. How the Transition will be Managed document.

3. Workstream Terms of Reference documents.

4. How the Transition will be Signed-off document.

Each of these are described in more detail below.

How the Transition will be Governed Document

The purpose of this document is to provide a framework for how the Steering Group and Transition Managers will work together and steer the Transition towards a successful conclusion. The document is divided into four sections:

1. A description of the three levels of Governance and what their roles are: Steering Group, Transition Managers and Workstream Leads.

2. A description of the Joint Governance meetings that will be held to monitor and steer progress.

3. An agreed calendar showing when Joint Governance meetings will be held.

4. A table identifying the Seller and Buyer Transition Teams.

This document is aimed at the Steering Group members and Transition Managers.

How the Transition will be Managed Document

This is a comprehensive document that describes how the Transition from Seller to Buyer will be managed. It contains critical information for Workstream Leads.

The document contains the following sections:

1. Transition Strategy. This section lists the Transition objectives and the principles outlining how the Transition teams should behave. It also gives an overview of the five Phases of the Transition.

2. Transition Programme Management. This section provides a summary of the Programme Management practices that will be used during the Transition.

3. Transition Workshops. This section gives an overview of each of the four Workshops that will be held during the Transition.

Workstream Terms of Reference Documents

All Workstream Leads will develop a Terms of Reference document. The document identifies such things as the Scope of Work and Deliverables that the Workstream will complete during the Transition. These elements of the document will be used to generate the Transition Plan. The Terms of Reference documents also contain an initial estimate of Workstream resource requirements. These will feed into the initial Transition resource plan and 'bottom's up' Transition Budget.

The document contains the following sections:

1. Contact Information for Workstream Leads and Workstream team members.

2. Scopes of Work for the Workstream.

3. Deliverables and Key Interdependencies with other Workstreams.

4. What work is considered 'out of scope' for the Workstream.

5. Workstream Resource and Budget Estimates for Buyer and Seller.

6. How the Workstream team will work together.

7. Any other points for consideration.

How the Transition will be Signed-off Document

Another essential document to agree and write down is *How the Transition will be Signed-off*. This document needs to align with any wording that has been incorporated into the Sale and Purchase Agreement or the Transfer of Operatorship Agreement.

The document typically comprises the following two sections:

1. Confirmation about who will sign-off that all Category A Deliverables have been completed. This is normally a two-step process: the Workstream Leads firstly sign-off to say that their Workstream's Category A Deliverables have been completed; then the Transition Managers sign-off to say that all the Transition Category A Deliverables have been completed.

2. Confirmation about who will sign-off that Operatorship can transfer safely from Seller to Buyer. This is normally done by the Transition Managers; however, some Steering Groups have requested the incumbent and future Operations Managers to sign-off.

9. Transition Service Agreements

In some instances, the Seller may need to enter into a contractual arrangement with the Buyer for a limited number of services to continue being provided until sometime in the future.

From a practical perspective, the shorter the duration of the Transition, the higher the number of Transition Service Agreements that are likely to be required. However, for long term ease and simplicity my bias is to try and minimise the number of contractual arrangements that are put in place.

The Transition Management Team should set up and manage a Transition Service Agreement Tracker. This will typically contain the following information:

- Title of the Agreement.
- High-level Scope of the Agreement.
- Duration of the Agreement.
- Cost structure of the Agreement.
- Buyer and Seller sponsors or focal points.

Further Assistance

To make your life simpler, you may wish to avail yourself of the following products and services. Details of these can be found at:

www.matrixxsolutions.com

For any and all our sessions and activities, our Trainers will be happy to sign Non-Disclosure Agreements with you, enabling you to talk freely about your Transition.

Fully editable set of Transition Documentation

We have created a fully editable set of Transition materials that you can use to get your Transition off to a flying start.

All materials are consistent with this book.

The full set of materials includes:

- Generic Stakeholder Communication Plan.
- *How the Transition will be Governed* document.
- *How the Transition will be Managed* document.
- Generic Workstream Terms of Reference documents.
- *How the Transition will be Signed-off* document.
- Full presentation for Kick-Off Workshop.
- Full presentation for Plan Review Workshop.
- Full presentation for Mid-Transition Review Workshop.
- Full presentation for Operational Readiness Workshop.
- Blank Transition Risk Register.
- Blank Transition Progress Report.
- Blank Transition Service Agreement Tracker.
- And more…

Provision of Training Courses

We recognise that not everyone has had prior experience of Transitions. To help you 'get up the learning curve', we offer the following two courses:

'An Executive's Guide to Transitions'

This one day interactive course is aimed at Steering Group members, Transition Managers and Transition Management Leads.

Our experienced Trainers will take you through each stage of the Transition and bring it to life for you.

This course is ideal for Buyer and Seller Transition Teams to attend prior to announcing the Sale and Purchase of assets. It enables you to start building a relationship between the Transition Teams and provides you an opportunity to collectively agree how your Transition will be governed and managed.

'A Workstream Lead's Guide to Transitions'

This one day interactive course is aimed at Transition Management Team members and Workstream Leads. It provides a comprehensive overview of a Transition.

Depending on your needs, we can also bring former Workstream Leads into this training course, to share their experience of Transition.

Facilitation of Transition Workshops

The four Workshops that take place throughout the course of the Transition are critical events. You will want to ensure that these run as smoothly as possible.

Our experienced Facilitators will work with you to:

- Tailor the Workshop materials to your Transition.
- Facilitate your Workshop, enabling you to focus on contributing to the event.
- Issue you with a set of actions and decisions taken at the Workshop, for your use.

External Input and Support to your Transition

There may be times throughout your Transition when the Steering Group wish to get external input or you may find it difficult to source suitable internal candidates to fulfil the roles of Transition Manager, Transition Management Team Lead or Workstream Lead.

We have an extensive list of Associates, comprising former Transition Managers, Transition Management Team Leads and Workstream Leads, who can support you.

Email us to discuss your requirements, at info@matrixxsolutions.com or fill in a web-form at www.matrixxsolutions.com/contact-us

About the Author

Roger has extensive experience of the Oil and Gas Industry, having worked in that sector for over twenty-five years. He is based out of the UK but enjoys working on projects all over the world.

After a long career with super-major BP, Roger launched his own consultancy, Matrixx Solutions Ltd. It builds on his areas of expertise:

- Transitioning assets from one company to another.
- Improving business performance through Operations Excellence.
- Change Management (particularly focusing on helping companies deliver their change vision).
- Providing practical Oil and Gas Operational support.

He is married and has three children who keep him young. Integrity and honesty are important to him, as well as operating in excellence.

Glossary of Terms and Abbreviations

Business Continuity Plan	During the Drive to Completion Phase, there will be a period when applications are not available to the end-user: whilst the IT team are extracting data from the Seller's system and making it available on the Buyer's system. During this time, Workstream Leads will need to have Business Continuity Plans in place. These describe what alternate actions need to be taken, or processes that need to be followed, to enable the business to continue running.
Category A Deliverable	Deliverables that must be completed prior to Completion taking place, or are essential for the Transfer to take place on the designated date.
Category B Deliverable	Deliverables that may be completed after Completion Date.
Close Out Phase	This Phase commences once Cutover has been completed.
COMAH	Control of Major Accident Hazards – UK legislation governing onshore major hazard sites.
Communications Specialist	The person who helps retain the support and enthusiasm of employees and others affected by the Transition. They are members of the Transition Management Team.
Completion Date (*)	Means the date on which all the paperwork is signed/executed that actually effects the transfer of legal and beneficial interests/ownership rights.
Conditions precedent (*)	Are those conditions that must be met before Completion Date.
Cutover Plan	A very detailed step by step Plan showing what needs to be done to power up the Buyer's infrastructure and applications, switch over (or cutover) the Seller's systems to the Buyer's systems, and then power down the Seller's systems.
Data Room (*)	Means either a physical location or a virtual site in which information related to the asset for sale is made available in confidence to prospective

	Buyers.
Deliverable Run-Down Curve	One of the standard reports that is published by the Transition Planner. It has two lines: the first one shows the target profile of Deliverable completion; the second one shows the actual profile of Deliverable completion. By comparing the two lines, you can see whether Deliverable completion is ahead or behind schedule.
Delivery Phase	The Delivery Phase of the Transition commences once the Workstream Leads have had time to sufficiently develop their Workstream Plans. It starts with a Plan Review Workshop.
Drive to Completion Phase	This Phase of the Transition commences after the Mid-Transition Review Workshop has been held. During this Phase, the Category A Deliverables are progressively closed out by the Workstream Leads and the focus turns to becoming Operationally ready.
Freeze Calendar	A calendar which gives a day by day visualisation of the period leading up to Completion Date when IT Applications will be 'frozen', 'loading' or 'live'.
Go/No-Go Decision Meeting	Prior to Completion Date, a critical decision needs to be made: whether to progress with Completion on the planned date or not. This decision needs to be formally taken by the Steering Group members at the Go/No-Go Decision Meeting.
High Level Strategic Plan	One of the standard reports that is published by the Transition Planner. This report is a high level, visual summary of the critical milestones and Deliverables through the life cycle of the Transition. It shows which ones have been completed and if any have slipped. It is commonly used by the Steering Group to review progress of the Transition.
How the Transition will be Governed document	The purpose of this document is to provide a framework for how the Steering Group and Transition Managers will work together and steer the Transition towards a successful conclusion.

	This document is aimed at the Steering Group members and Transition Managers.
How the Transition will be Managed document	This is a comprehensive document that describes how the Transition from Seller to Buyer will be managed. It describes the Transition Strategy, Programme Management elements and gives an overview of the Transition Workshops. It contains critical information for Workstream Leads.
Initiation & Ramp Up Phase	This Phase of The Transition commences as soon as the Sale and Purchase Agreement has been signed.
'in the know'	Those individuals who are aware that the Transaction is progressing. These people will normally have signed a Confidentiality Letter or Non-Disclosure Agreement restricting them from disclosing information to any person or company that is not 'in the know'.
Joint Steering Group Meeting	This meeting enables the Steering Group to monitor progress of the Transition and steer it towards a successful conclusion. It is attended by the Steering Group and Transition Managers. Its purpose is to review progress, provide oversight of 'red' risks, ratify the plan, and deal with issues that have been raised by the Transition Managers. The meetings are typically held monthly.
Joint Transition Management Team Meeting	This meeting provides a formal opportunity for the Buyer's and Seller's Transition Management Teams to discuss progress and intervene where required. Its purpose is to resolve issues, review the Transition Plan, agree any interventions that need to be taken, and agree the agenda and contents of upcoming Workshops and Steering Group meetings. The meetings are typically held weekly.
Joint Transition Team Meeting	The focus of this meeting is on sharing context and direction from the Transition Management Team and highlighting and discussing cross-Workstream issues that need to be resolved. All members of the Buyer's and Seller's Transition Management Teams and all Workstream Leads

	attend this meeting. The meetings are typically held every two weeks.
Kick-Off Workshop	A Workshop that is held in the Initiation & Ramp Up Phase, once most of the Buyer and Seller Workstream Leads are available.
Knowledge Transfer	The sharing and transfer of ways of working, practices and procedures from Seller to Buyer.
Mid-Transition Review Workshop	An important event that is held during the Delivery Phase of the Transition. It is timed to occur at approximately the midpoint of the Transition.
Oil & Gas UK (*)	The UK Oil and Gas Industry Association trading as Oil & Gas UK (and formerly known as UKOOA).
Operational Readiness Workshop	The Operational Readiness Workshop is held in the Drive to Completion Phase of the Transition. The purpose of it is to get a clear understanding from Workstream Leads on their preparedness to sign-off their Category A Deliverables by Completion Date.
PLANC	Permits, Licences, Authorisations, Notifications and Consents.
Plan Review Workshop	A Workshop that is held during the Delivery Phase. The goal of the Workshop is to collaboratively review and challenge all Workstream Plans. From a behavioural perspective this is a critical event, where the intent is to change mindsets of Workstream Leads from 'Planning with a bit of Execution' to 'Focussed delivery of the Plan'.
Pre-announcement Preparation Phase	This Phase of the Transition commences at some point before the Sale and Purchase Agreement is signed and is usually cloaked in secrecy.
Pre-emption	Means a right to acquire certain property in preference to any other company.
Programme Management	A compilation of clear and simple practices that enable the Transition to progress through the five Phases, from Pre-announcement Preparation Phase to Close Out Phase. They cover: Transition Governance; Transition Planning; Transition

	Budgeting; Risk Management; Progress Reporting; Document Collaboration; Communications; Programme Management Documents and, Transition Service Agreements.
'ring-fence'	Means the legal 'walling off' of people, assets or liabilities within an organisation, to fix the scope of a sale or purchase.
Risk Register	A repository of risk information.
Rules of Engagement document	A document for people in the Seller's organisation that are going to be transferred to the Buyer but have an active role in the Transition. It defines what they can and cannot say and do.
Safety Case	The Offshore Installations (Safety Case) Regulations 2005, which aims to reduce the risks from major accident hazards to the health and safety of the workforce employed on offshore installations and connected activities.
Sale and Purchase Agreement (*)	Means the legal agreement between the Seller and the Buyer for the sale and purchase of an asset or assets.
Stakeholder Communication Plan	A Plan that details, minute by minute, who is going to communicate with all the impacted internal and external parties, once the sale and purchase is announced.
Steering Group	The first level of governance for the Transition. The Steering Group comprises of senior Executives from both the Seller and Buyer companies who steer the Transition to a successful outcome.
Transition	The process and activities led by the Transition Management Team, to transfer assets, data, personnel, processes and practices from the Seller to the Buyer.
Transition Administrator	A member of the Transition Management Team who performs an administrative role, to help the Transition progress smoothly.
Transition Budget	The overall Transition Budget is made up of the Seller Transition Budget and the Buyer Transition Budget. It provides an estimate of the total spend that will be incurred by both parties.

Transition Management Lead	The 'right hand' to the Transition Manager, who ensures that the Transition is progressing in accordance with 'How the Transition will be Governed' and 'How the Transition will be Managed' documents.
Transition Management Team	Each company will establish a Transition Management Team, comprising the following roles: Transition Manager, Transition Management Lead, Transition Planner (this role is shared between companies), Communications Specialist and Transition Administrator. The role of the Transition Management Team is to support the Transition Managers in delivering a successful Transition.
Transition Manager	The individuals appointed to manage the Transition from the point that the Sale and Purchase Agreement is signed to the Completion Date when the assets and Operatorship are formally taken over by the Buyer.
Transition Plan	The Transition Plan is a fully integrated set of well-defined, individual activities at Workstream level. The plan shows the activities and milestones that need to be completed to enable the Category A and B Deliverables to be signed off.
Transition Planner	A vital member of the Transition Management Team who ensures that an accurate Transition Plan is developed and maintained.
Transition Progress Report	A formal written report of progress, by Workstream, that is issued on a regular basis. For most transitions a two-weekly reporting cycle is sufficient.
Transition S-Curve	One of the standard reports that is published by the Transition Planner. The report has two lines: the first one is the baseline S-Curve which is flatter at the beginning and end but steeper in the middle. The second line represents actual progress against the baseline.
Transition Service Agreement	A contractual arrangement for a limited number of services to continue being provided by the Seller to the Buyer, after Completion Date.

TUPE	The Transfer of Undertakings (Protection of Employment) Regulations 2006. This is an important part of UK labour law and protects employees whose business is being transferred to another company.
Workstream	A tried and tested way of organising the Transition. Workstreams are established to identify and transfer all the Seller's people, processes, tools, systems, data and assets to the Buyer as quickly and effectively as possible.
Workstream Budget	The Workstream Budget is made up of the Seller Workstream Budget and the Buyer Workstream Budget. These provide an estimate of the total spend that will be incurred by the Workstream by the respective companies.
Workstream Lead	The individual appointed to transition all the defined scope within their area of responsibility from Seller to Buyer within the specified timeline.

Source: The asterisked (*) terms used on the Glossary of Terms and Abbreviations were extracted from *Guidelines for Best Practice for Managing Information Transfer at the Time of Asset Sales* document published by CDA, part of Oil and Gas UK in September 2013.

15999721R00074

Printed in Great Britain
by Amazon